The 18-Footer Britannia

100 years of a Sydney Icon

Sydney
WOODEN BOAT
School
www.sydneywoodenboatschool.com.au

Britannia works upwind towards the Sow and Pigs on a hazy day.
HALL COLLECTION ANMM

The 18-Footer Britannia

100 years of a Sydney Icon

Ian Hugh Smith

Sydney
WOODEN BOAT
School

Also by the author:

The Open Boat: The Origin, Evolution and Construction of the Australian 18-Footer

Wooden Boatbuilding: The Sydney Wooden Boat School Manuals

Published by Sydney Wooden Boat School
www.sydneywoodenboatschool.com.au

Copyright Ian Hugh Smith 2020

ISBN: 978-0-6481-386-3-1

Design and layout by Tricia Smith

All reasonable efforts were taken to obtain permission to use copyright material reproduced in this book, but in some cases copyright could not be traced. The author welcomes information in this regard.

Printed by Ingram Spark

Front cover image framed William Hall photo presented to author by the family of crewman Jack Halliday. Back cover top: Hall photo in author's collection. Bottom: Phil Moore.

Contents

Introduction		6
Chapter 1:	*Britannia* Joins the Fleet	7
Chapter 2:	The Early Sailing Years	24
Chapter 3:	Champion!	37
Chapter 4:	Football	42
Chapter 5:	The Great Depression and the Split	46
Chapter 6:	The Later Years	52
Chapter 7:	The Post War Years	64
Chapter 8:	Restoration and Revival	72
Appendix I:	Boats Built by John Robinson Jnr and Wee Georgie Robinson	84
Appendix II:	Wee Georgie and his Model Boats	90
Appendix III:	*Britannia's* Crew	92
Bibliography		96
Acknowledgements		99

Author's Note:
Many of the images reprinted here are unfortunately of low quality, many being from newspapers and some from micro-filmed reproductions. I have included them when no better images, or no images at all are available of a particular person, boat or event. Some have also been previously published in my book *The Open Boat*.

Introduction

This is not just the story of a boat, or of the man who built it, but of a community and of a sport that played a huge role in our society in the first half of the twentieth century in Sydney. If you were a young fit resident of any of Sydney's waterfront working-class suburbs like North Sydney, Woolloomooloo, The Rocks, Pyrmont, Glebe or Balmain, on Saturdays you went racing in open boats with your relatives and workmates in Summer, and played football (most often the new code Rugby League since 1908) often with the same relatives and workmates in the Winter. Crowds filled the multiple ferries that followed the fleet, picking up from wharves around Balmain and the city, and thousands more watched from headlands, particularly Bradley's Head which was known as Scotchman's Hill. Gambling was common in spite of it being illegal. Newspapers devoted many columns to race reports. The leading skippers were as famous as leading footballers were.

George Robinson was one of these men. From a sailing family he was a star of both 18-footer racing and of Rugby League and was a shipwright by trade. He designed, built and raced *Britannia* for 23 seasons over 25 years, taking part in about 650 races winning 40 of them including 14 Championships. After her racing career *Britannia* became a launch until Wee Georgie began to restore her in the 1980's intending to donate her to the Sydney Heritage Fleet, but died before completion in 1987. The new Australian National Maritime Museum (ANMM) made *Britannia* their first acquisition and restored her for display, and she has been on proud display for most of the period from 1990 until now. *Britannia*'s career tells the story of a significant part of our maritime heritage and of the 18-footer community.

Three generations of Robinsons, Ron, Jack and George.
THE SUN, SUNDAY
MAR 5 1939 TROVE NLA

Chapter 1

Britannia Joins the Fleet

Britannia (far left with Red Duster on sail) starts her first race in the Sydney Sailing Club Championship on 8 November 1919. *Britannia* was fourth. The winner was *Scot,* far right.   SCRAPBOOK SFS COLLECTION

On Saturday the 8th of November 1919 a new eighteen-footer joined a fleet of twenty others for the Championship of the Sydney Sailing Club, one of two clubs conducting races for 18-footers. Skipper and builder George Robinson, known to all as Wee Georgie from his career as the Balmain Tigers First Grade Rugby League halfback, had a reasonable start and worked his way through the field in a moderate Nor'Easter. At one point the boat filled up, taking on a great deal of water before rounding the "new light" at the Sow and Pigs reef, the first top mark. This would have slowed them down until bailed out by hand, but they still managed to get 4th place in the race.

This was remarked on at the time as being a commendable effort, largely because brand-new boats at the time generally needed a good few races to "work up" the boat and crew, but it was no great surprise to anyone as George came from a sailing family and was already a Champion sailor in another class. George's father was John "Jack" Robinson with a history of winning in 18-footers and before that in 22- and 24-footers. Jack never owned a 22- or 24-footer, but was a sought-after skipper in the 1890's. With large prize money on offer from Regatta committees and the new clubs, the Johnstones Bay Sailing Club (JBSC) and the Sydney Flying Squadron (SFS), owners of boats were keen to get the best skippers, and Jackie Robinson was one of a select group of proven race-winners who would be promised a share of the prize money. He was in the company of men like Chris Webb, George Ellis, Billy Read, Fred Doran, George Holmes Senior and Junior and Thomas Colebrook Senior and Junior. He had sailed his self-built 14-footer *Young Jack* to victory in enough races in the 1880's to attract the attention of the big boat owners. The first big boat he is found skippering was the 22-footer *Atalanta* built by Hubbard of Glebe Point in 1889, which he steered with success that season including second place in the inaugural race of the new JBSC in January 1891. The next season he moved over to the 24-footer *Volunteer,* also built by Hubbard in 1889 and was associated with this boat until at least 1897, winning a number of championships and many handicap races. He had other shorter-term relationships with the 22-footer *Marvel,* as well as the 22-footers *Ellie, Figtree* and *Vigilant*.

George's older brother John Junior was a boatbuilder and built an 18-footer *Young Jack* in 1906 for his father (who almost certainly helped in construction) and *Zanita* in 1907 for Bill Martin (to Martin's design). John Jnr also sailed with his father and in 18's as for'd hand, including the visiting West Australian boat *Westana* in the famous gale of 1913 where *Westana* was the only boat to finish.

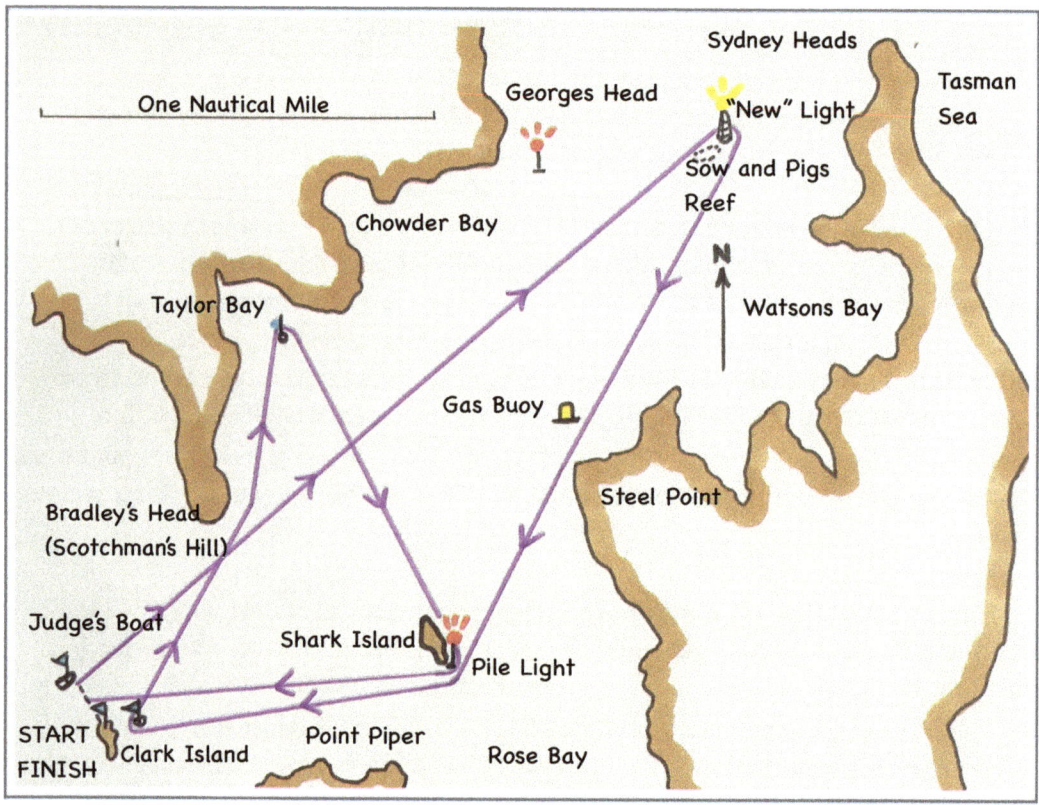

The Number One or Championship course, or Sow and Pigs course which varied little from the 1890's until 1942. The same course was sailed regardless of the wind direction. It was about nine nautical miles in straight lines. One variation was the George's Head Light course which went around the George's Head light and the Gas buoy instead of the Sow and Pigs. The Sydney Flying Squadron sailed short triangles for their fortnightly 2 heats and final races which varied but mostly started at Clark and went around the Gas buoy and Shark Island pile light to finish at Clark. Occasionally a buoy would be laid in Rose Bay as the South-Eastern mark instead of the pile light. Overall Harbour map page 83.

Jack Senior was a blacksmith by trade but he was a boatbuilder by inclination and after campaigning *Young Jack* for two seasons built another 18, *Livonia* in 1908, and sailed her for four seasons. Wee Georgie sailed often in the crew of *Livonia*, but he was also a skipper in his own boat, a 6-footer he had named *Britannia* and built in 1915.

Livonia, Jack's second 18-footer he built and campaigned for four seasons. George often sailed in her as a teenager.
HALL COLLECTION ANMM

Volunteer, the 24-footer George's father Jack steered for many seasons in the 1890's.
HALL COLLECTION ANMM

Wee Georgie sailed his 6-footer *Britannia* with the 6-footer fleet at the Balmain Dingy Sailing Club, and was the Club Champion three seasons in a row. In five seasons sailing the 6-footer Wee Georgie won 29 races and had 36 seconds and 35 thirds, and won the point score four years in a row.

George with his 6-footer *Britannia*. ANMM

George's first Club Championship medallion for 1916-17 season.
SFS COLLECTION
DONATED BY MILLER FAMILY

The obverse of the medallion

The 6-footer *Britannia* in which George won 29 races including three Club Championships.
A APPLETON COLLECTION
AHSSA

Wee Georgie Robinson about 1919. SFS PROGRAMME

The new 18-footer *Britannia* was reported as being prepared for the season in October of 1919, with some newspapers attributing the build to Jack Robinson, some to George, and some to both. It is certain that George did most of the work with some degree of assistance from his father and brother. *Britannia* was built in the shed of brother John who had been an officer in the Australian Flying Corps in England during the War and had set up as a boatbuilder at 8 School St Balmain East (on the waterfront). George and occasionally Jack Snr worked for him at this point. They were expected to be ready a week or two before they finally appeared on 8 November. It is not known if they actually launched the boat before the first race day. *Britannia* was reported as carrying the rig and sails of *Livonia* in the first race at launching, which seems probable, but they had replaced *Livonia*'s six-pointed red star with the Red Duster.

Why would Wee Georgie have called his boat(s) *Britannia*? In modern Australia we tend to forget that in 1919 virtually every Australian considered themselves British. In fact, technically they were, there was no such thing as Australian citizenship until 1949! And also there was a well-established tradition of naming boats after famous British and American racing yachts such as *Volunteer, Vigilant,* and *Genesta*. The Royal racing cutter *Britannia* launched in 1893 was still actively sailing in 1919. Naming his tiny 6-footer after the Royal cutter may have been a bit of irony.

As part of the fact of considering themselves British, several 18-footers named *Australian* had used the Union Jack as their sail insignia. Possibly because this insignia was already taken, Wee Georgie used the British red ensign, the Red Duster as his sail insignia on both the 6- and 18-footer *Britannias.* As Sydney's leading vexillologist John Vaughan has pointed out, the Red Duster  was one of the most recognisable flags on Earth in 1919, as it was carried by a huge merchant fleet and seen in almost every port in the world. Ready-made flags were a common choice for sail insignias, *Golding* carried the P&O house flag, *Mascotte* carried the Australian Union Steamship Navigation Company house flag.

The Sydney Flying Squadron and the Sydney Sailing Club

During the 1890's sailing for open boats of 18' and up was run by the Johnstones Bay Sailing Club (instituted in late 1890) and the Sydney Flying Squadron (1891). The clubs cooperated so that their fixtures did not clash, and they eventually settled on running races on alternate Saturdays. SFS races apart from Championships were almost all run in two heats and a final, the front half of each fleet entering the final, around a short triangular course which varied but started and finished North-West of Clark Island and mostly stayed to the North and East of the Island. The JBSC ran long course races, in fact quite long by later standards, a race was often 3 hours. They started and finished their races in Johnstones Bay which name has faded from modern maps, but it is still in the water between Pyrmont and Balmain just West of the city. Their courses went as far as Shark Island and even Manly. In February 1899 a new club was formed, the Sydney Sailing Club (SSC) with some big backers such as Sam Hordern (of the Anthony Hordern's department stores) and ran a few races in the remainder of that season, open to all classes. There may have been personality clashes with JBSC officials who accused the SSC of setting up in opposition to them. Before the 1899-1900 season started the JBSC published their intended programme after refusing to consult with the other clubs. In September the NSW Sailing Council set up a three-way conference which resulted in a time-sharing agreement with each of four clubs (they included the Sydney Dingy Club) having exclusive dates on which no other club could charter steamers. JBSC got 5 dates, SFS 9, SSC 7 and SDC 3.

A September 1900 conference established a similar regime for the 1900-1901 season and the JBSC decided to conduct events only for the dingy classes, 14's, 10's and 8-footers, but it all fell apart in November when the JBSC withdrew from the NSW Sailing Council. The SFS and SSC were now left as the only two clubs running races for the 18 and 22-footers. They continued their programmes which didn't occupy every Saturday that season, but for the 1901-02 season they divided 18 Saturdays from October to March, 10 for the SFS and 7 for the SSC and one joint race. In subsequent seasons they filled up every Saturday alternately, with occasional joint races, and this regime held until 1925, the SFS races still two heats and a final, and the SSC long course races.

The Sydney Flying Squadron and Sydney Sailing Club Honour Board from WWI. ADRIENNE JACKSON

The fleets of the Sydney Flying Squadron and the Sydney Sailing Club had continued racing each season through the War and the fleet numbers were relatively constant at around 19-21 boats racing each week, but crew was more difficult to find as so many young men had gone off to War. The joint Sydney Flying Squadron and Sydney Sailing Club Honour Board shows 149 members who served, and of 109 whose stories have been traced by Adrienne Jackson and Steve and Veronica Scully (see Bibliography), 27 (25%) did not return, and 49 (45%) were wounded.

Only three new boats were built during the War years, contrasting with four or five boats per year for several years before that. *Britannia* was the only new 18-footer in Sydney in the 1919-20 season. Possibly the flu pandemic influenced this. Of the 20 other boats in the fleet on 8 November 1919, only three were under five years old, ten

Scot built by Donnelly in 1906 won the SSC Championship of 1919 which was the first race *Britannia* entered, and was steered by Jack Smith.
HALL COLLECTION ANMM

had been built between 1908 and 1913 and seven were built between 1898 and 1907. But all of the most competitive boats were amongst the older two groups. Here are the boats in *Britannia's* first race:

Scot	1906 steered by Jack Smith won the race.
Golding	1910 a former Australian Champion. Second in the race under Rocko Beashel.
Mascotte	launched as *Nimrod* in 1909 and a champion under that name. Third in the race under WJ "Billy" Duncan.
Kismet	1912 a former SFS and State Champion, steered by Billy Dunn.
Federal	1898 owned and steered by Orlando Taylor.
Pastime	1910 Sam Richardson.
Mavis	1904 FW Moppett, won the previous Australian Championship.
Moyana	1914 WC "Trappy" Duncan.
Mississippi	launched as *Admiral* in 1913, R Budnick.
HC Press	1913 George Press.
Arline	launched as *Eileen* in 1907, Bill Fisher.
Donnelly	1898 a consistent prize winner, C Newman.
Advance	1909 "Happy" Harry Thompson.
Swastika	1913 Bill Edney.
Onda	1916 JM Firth.
Rocket	1915 Tom Tait.
Mona	1905 G King.
Florrie	launched as *Acme* 1906 I Pont.
Hero	1911 G Degan.
Sunny South	1909 H Rodrick.
Sydney	launched as *Eunice* 1908, Norm Blackman.
Desdemona	1912 AC Roberts.

(*Sydney* and *Desdemona* had both nominated for the race but did not start.)

Also missing was pre-war Champion *Australian (III)*, which the great Chris Webb had steered to several Championship wins. *Australian* had not raced for almost 3 years after Webb did not pull off the course when disqualified. Owner Watty Ford was "outed" after objecting at the next sailing meeting. Commodore Mark Foy urged Ford to retract but he vowed he would not race *Australian* again and would sell her. True to his word, he did just that.

Golding built by Billy Golding in 1910 was second under Rocko Beashel. Notice the knot tied at the head of the balloon jib to allow it to fit a shorter mast.
HARRY THOMPSON COLLECTION SFS

Mascotte launched as *Nimrod* in 1909 was third under Billy Duncan.
HARRY THOMPSON COLLECTION SFS

Kismet built in 1912 by Charlie Dunn was a former and future Champion that *Britannia* beat on the day, under Billy Dunn.
SFS COLLECTION

Donnelly, built by Joe Donnelly in 1898 was no slouch in 1919 in spite of her age, but was beaten on the day by *Britannia*, under C Newman.
HALL COLLECTION ANMM

Championships and Handicaps

Most races during the season were handicap starts, whether they were short-course races of two heats and a final or long-course races. Each boat was allocated a handicap in minutes or quarters of a minute which indicated the start it had over the scratch boat, ie the slower boats started first. Those with bigger handicaps were referred to as the long-markers. In the 1920's handicaps were usually set by one man, the official handicapper, but owners could protest their handicap at the weekly meeting, though they were not often successful.

There were several Championship races each season, varying between four and six. Each of the two clubs had a Club Championship, there was always a State Championship and in most years an Australian Championship, and a Port Jackson Championship. Every Championship was decided on one race. Championships were always long-course races and starts were scratch starts, ie all boats started together.

New 18-footer building resumed in 1921 when five new boats appeared, with six more the following year, and the fleet began to grow. But first we need to discuss where the 18-footers came from.

Origin and Evolution of 18-footers

I have dealt with this thoroughly in *The Open Boat-The Origin, Evolution and Construction of the Australian 18-Footer*, but here's a summary. Folklore told us that the 18-footers evolved from working boats, but the truth is a bit more complex. The 18-footers themselves were never working boats, they were exclusively a racing class. But they evolved from the previously dominant racing class the 22-footers, which in turn evolved from the racing class of 24-footers which had started off as fishing boats in the 1870's, with some input from fleets of racing skiffs which developed in the 1870's from working watermen's skiffs.

The first recognisable 18-footers appeared in the early 1890's as smaller versions of the then-dominant 24-footers, which were soon surpassed by the 22-footers largely due to the impetus of Intercolonial competition between Sydney and Brisbane in the mid to late 1890's. The 22's only remained dominant for a few seasons after the Intercolonial contests stopped in 1899. By 1902 the 18-footers were the dominant class, judging by the amount of coverage in newspapers and the relative amount of prize money offered by regattas.

It helped that Sydney's leading skipper of the 1890's Chris Webb decided to spend most of his time at the helm of the 18-footer *Australian* built by Sam Williams in 1896 and owned by Watty Ford who was the second generation of owners of a large ship and boatbuilding yard in Berry's Bay (now the site of Noakes boatyard). Other leading skippers found their way onto other 18-footers to challenge him. The crowds turned out to watch, paying to get on ferries that followed the fleet and indulging in considerable gambling.

New 18-footers were built every year. Three to five boats were built each year from 1901 to 1904, then nine in 1905 and 12 in 1906. Some of the early 18's were relatively narrow: *Aztec* 1892, *Ariel 1894* and *Zena* as late as 1905 were under 7' beam. But as the 22's had got wider and wider, the same thing happened to the 18's. *Yvonne* 1895 and *Australia (I)* 1898 were both 8' beam, *Kyeewa* and *Donnelly* both 1898 were 8'4". Not in every case however. Boatbuilder Charlie Dunn in particular continued to build narrow boats, mostly for himself, as well as a few beamier boats for customers. *Crescent IV* was 6' beam, several others were 7' or under, but his *Kismet, Avalon, Endeavour* and *Mele Bilo II* were either side of 7'6". He built a total of eight 18-footers named *Crescent* and sailed them for a season or two and then sold them on, often to fishermen at Crescent Head on the North Coast where he had family connections.

Although we commonly hear the 18-footers referred to as skiffs, this only began in the 1930's. Before that the 18-footers were referred to simply as 18-footers, or

Lady Loch 1893 by Reid, one of the big-beam 24-footers, and one of the last ones built. HALL COLLECTION ANMM

occasionally as dinghy-type 18-footers to distinguish them from more skiff-like 18-footers that made an appearance every now and again. In the 19th Century there had been three classes of racing skiffs that evolved from watermen's skiffs which were the water taxis of Sydney Harbour. The classes were 16-foot, 19-foot and 22-foot skiffs, every class sharing the same maximum beam of five feet, and maximum depth of 20 inches. This narrow beam and shallow depth was what distinguished skiffs from other boats. The 22-foot skiffs died out after only a few seasons in the 1870's, the 19-foot skiffs in the 1880's. The 16-foot skiffs lasted until the mid-to late 1890's. In 1901 a group of sailors got together and established a new club to sail skiffs up to 16-foot in length and 5'6" beam, with limited boom length to restrict sail area. Of course some experimenters built ridiculous rigs with super-long gaffs and even lateen rigs in the first few seasons, until the club put a limit on sail area in 1904. The new class built up numbers rapidly until by 1910 there were 27 boats on the register and clubs had been started in other areas. And in spite of their limited sail area, these skiffs were fast. This did not go unnoticed by some 18-footer sailors.

In 1906, newspapers were full of rumours that several 18-footers were being built that were narrow and more skiff-like. Owners of the big-beam boats felt threatened by

Aztec 1892 by Hubbard, one of the earliest 18-footers. They carried all the sails of their bigger sisters. ROBIN ELLIOTT COLLECTION

this, their chief public argument being that the crowds came to see the big-beam boats and their clouds of sail and would not turn up to see smaller boats and rigs. As it happened, only one of these boats appeared for the 1906-07 season, and it happened to be *Young Jack*, built by Jack Robinson for himself. The boat had a beam of seven feet. The Sydney Sailing Club promptly banned any boats seven feet or under, but the Sydney Flying Squadron did not. This meant that Jack could only sail *Young Jack* with the Sydney Flying Squadron, every second week. He did so, without a great deal of success and the powers that be felt relieved. In 1908 he gave up and built the beamier *Livonia*.

But a successful 16-foot skiff sailor named Horace Rodrick tried it again in 1907 with a boat he got Donnelly to build named *Oweenee* after his successful 16-foot skiff of that name. This boat caused more upset than had *Young Jack* because it won a couple of Championship races. But largely because of the difficulties with club officials (they would not allow him to compete for the Australian Championship) Rodrick gave up sailing *Oweenee* and went back to 16-footers.

The owners of the big boats relaxed and were not troubled again until 1932, but more on this later.

On the eve of World War One the two Clubs were enjoying a golden age with regular fleets of 19-21 boats and huge patronage on the ferries. This enabled them to offer prizes of £15 for a win in a regular handicap race down to £1 for 6th place which allowed most boats, sometimes all the boats in the fleet, to earn some money. The leading prize winners were taking home £80 or more in a season, at a time when a tradesman's wage was approximately £4 per week.

The start of the Interstate Championship on 3 February 1912. Jack Robinson's *Livonia* at right got the best of the start but ended up 5th. I have identified most of the boats on the FLEETS Page on the Open Boat website. HARRY THOMPSON COLLECTION SFS

But there were indications that things might be about to change and several newspaper commentators discussed this. A number of the leading skippers retired in this period, notably George Holmes and Tom Colebrook. Several leading boatbuilders also retired: Joe Donnelly built his last boat in 1914 and George Ellis and Billy Golding who were leading boatbuilders **and** skippers both retired, Golding not building a boat after 1913 and Ellis moving to Vancouver, Canada in 1907. But Charlie Dunn and Charlie Hayes continued to run their families' boatbuilding businesses, and Bill Fisher of the LaPerouse boatbuilding family had begun to make a name for himself as a skipper as well as a boatbuilder.

It turned out that nothing much changed. Throughout the 1920's new boats continued to be added to the fleet, and they were almost all big-beam boats. And the skippers' names were mostly familiar to people who had followed the fleet before the War. Chris Webb came back from retirement to steer the new *HC Press II* from the 1922-23 season. Lan Taylor bought Norman Wright's Brisbane boat *Thelma III* in 1920 and renamed her *Keriki* after his old 22-footer. Bill Fisher built *Australia* in 1921 and steered it himself. Stalwarts of the pre-War scene had new boats built: Happy Harry Thompson sold the 1909 *Advance* and had Sam Williams build him a new boat named *NSW* in 1922, using the same coat-of-arms insignia he'd used on *Advance;* Gordon and Stan King sold the 1905 *Mona* and had Charlie Dunn build them *Avalon* in 1922.

The fleets steadily grew, the two clubs continued to take turns to run races and ferry patrons continued to turn up and both clubs were prosperous.

Keriki Norman Wright, launched as *Thelma III* in 1918, joined the Sydney fleet in 1920. THE AUSTRALIAN MOTOR BOAT AND YACHTING MONTHLY, OCTOBER 1925

Australia Bill Fisher 1921. HARRY THOMPSON COLLECTION SFS

HC Press (II) George Press 1922. HARRY THOMPSON COLLECTION SFS

NSW Sam Williams 1922.
HARRY THOMPSON
COLLECTION SFS

Avalon Charlie Dunn 1922.
HARRY THOMPSON
COLLECTION SFS

Chapter 2

The Early Sailing Years

Wee Georgie and *Britannia* struggled to find form in the next races in November and December 1919. They finished 9th out of only 12 boats to finish in a gale in the SFS Championship on 29 November which is a bit of an achievement, but were 16th out of 20 in the State Championship on 20 December. They finally started to find form in January and February.

Britannia was 2nd in the Snails Bay Regatta on New Years Day 1920, and then won the first heat of the SFS race on 17 January off 2 minutes, but couldn't repeat it in the final. The Anniversary Regatta on 26 January had both a morning and afternoon race for 18-footers and Wee Georgie was 2nd in the morning race and 3rd in the afternoon race in a black Nor'easter winning a total of £8. A 3rd on 7 February was followed by his first full win on 14 February in a fresh Nor'easter off 3¾ minutes and he took home £12. Several more placings in February and March netted him a total of £48 for the SFS and SSC races which was mid-field in the list of earnings, plus around £10 or £12 in regattas. This was at a time when the cost of a new 18-footer was estimated at around £200, so he won approximately 30% of the value of his boat in the first season. At the time George was working as a boatbuilder for his brother John Junior at 8 School St Balmain East, and wages were likely to have been only a few pounds a week.

Soon after the start in the SFS Championship 29 November 1919, *Britannia's* fourth ever race. They were 9th. And yes, there was a boat called *Swastika*, long before the ancient symbol became sullied. THE SUN 30 NOV 1919 TROVE NLA

Britannia and *Kismet* waiting at Clark Island for the start on 25 September 1920 at the start of *Britannia's* second season. *Kismet* is closest with the blue Commonwealth flag with stars, *Britannia's* Red Duster has no stars. SYDNEY MAIL 29 SEP 1920, TROVE NLA

Britannia started her second season promisingly with a dead heat for third in the first race in a cold Southerly and a second in a heat in the second race. They won another heat in a race in late November but "filled up" and retired in another, and then had their first swim on 11 December rounding Shark Island for the second time.

Britannia did well enough in the three test races for selection for the Australian Championship, including a second place in the third test race on 15 January 1921 (pictured p27) to be selected along with *Mascotte*, *Kismet* and *HC Press* to represent NSW. The Championship race (all Championships were decided over one race at that time) was held the following week on Sydney Harbour with the four NSW boats racing against two from Queensland and two from Western Australia. It was won by *Vision* from Queensland. *Britannia's* jib "split from top to bottom" and her sails were referred to as "a disgrace".

Furious takes a dive off Shark Island in 1929. This shot made the cover of the weekly Sydney Flying Squadron programme of 9 November 1929.

Capsizing near the Edwards

The mark East of Shark Island was the pile light, and in most breezes, especially the common Nor'easters was a gybe mark. With more than half of the boom extending beyond the tuck (transom) gybing an 18-footer was a dangerous manoeuvre, and capsizes were common. The nearest beach to pull the boat up on to bail out (they could not be righted afloat) is Lady Martin's beach just downwind from the mark and is the home of the Royal Prince Edward Yacht Club. At some stage a tradition developed whereby a Club member or member of staff would bring a tray of glasses of rum down to the beach for the distressed mariners. I'm happy to say this tradition still holds for the 21st Century replica fleet.

Unidentified boat in the drink at the gybe mark.
HALL COLLECTION ANMM

Close to the finish of the third test race for the Australian Championships on 15 January 1921. *Britannia* (at right) was third.
AUTHOR'S COLLECTION

The start of the Australian Championship the very next week. *Britannia* (second right in the distance) was selected for NSW but split her jib during the race. It was won by *Vision* (Queensland) just left of centre with the crescent logo.   AUTHOR'S COLLECTION, SUPPLIED BY JIM COX, ROCKHAMPTON

More bad luck followed a few weeks later when *Britannia* broke her mast off Steel Point in a strong Southerly, but George either repaired the mast within a week or used a different rig because they raced the next Saturday and finished 4th off 1½ minutes. Also in this period they won the double of a heat and the final, and won another long course race which brought them into scratch for the last race of the season on 19 March, but they were unplaced. Total winnings for the season was £57, better than mid-field. I'm guessing he spent some of the money on a new mast and new sails, but maybe not.

Britannia seems to have won the start in this sequence from a Championship race from 1922. There are many images of Championship starts but there was usually only 4 to 6 of these starts per season out of 25-28 races. All others were staggered starts, boats took their handicap at the start so whoever was first across the line was the winner.
TOP PHOTO HALL COLLECTION, ANMM. BOTTOM PHOTO HARRY THOMPSON COLLECTION SFS

The third season was another promising one, *Britannia* winning one long course race and several heats, but getting into a lot of places and keeping their handicap low, mostly under a minute. They had their second swim early in the season. They got 4th in the SSC Championship race in early November and 2nd in the SFS Championship race in late November. Total prize winnings were £75, second only to *Mascotte* with £101.

Just before their fourth season started in September 1922 The Sun newspaper reported that *Britannia* had undergone alterations, raising the foredeck 9". I believe this to be false. As a boatbuilder, after close study of the hull I can see no evidence of this, in fact there is a lot of contrary evidence. But the newspaper also reported that *Britannia* was fitted with a new big main, 27' on the boom, 16' on the gaff, 16'6" hoist and 34' on the leech, which is more believable.

The fleet had grown with 26 boats regularly appearing in races. *Britannia* had no wins other than one heat, but still showed her capabilities by gaining 3rd place in the SFS Championship and 2nd in the SSC Championship. Their handicap fluctuated between ¼ minute and 1¾ minutes.

Britannia running square with second rig. HALL COLLECTION ANMM

Wee Georgie steered the boat in most races, but his father Jack steered at least once in each of the second, third and fourth seasons. Sometimes early and late in the season it was Wee Georgie's Rugby League commitments that caused his absence, but at the end of the fourth season he had to miss the last three races in March 1923 as he married Catherine Leishman on 10 March. Crewmate Mick Russell steered that day and obviously missed the wedding, and Jack Robinson the other two races, neither with any success.

A pre-season newspaper report in the Sunday Times of 12 August 1923 featured *Britannia's* "athletic crew". As well as George, the Balmain First Grade scrum half and Balmain League Swimming Club swimmer, there was the aforementioned Mick Russell another Balmain footballer and State swimming champion, Alf Frazer, a representative football player, Roy Liston of the Glebe 13 (Rugby League), E McFarlane, a trainer of the Balmain Club and Tony Russell of the undefeated reserve grade team of Balmain, later to be a first-grader and a champion skipper in his own right. *Britannia* was again mid-field in earnings that season, but kept their handicap under 2 minutes and often lower, and showed promise in gaining 2nd in both the SFS Championship and the State Championship.

Start of the SFS Championship 24 November 1923. ***Britannia*** is centre left with sail obscuring the ferry. They came 2nd. Wee Georgie was beginning to make a habit of being runner-up in Championships. POSTCARD IN GRAEME FERGUSON COLLECTION AHSSA

SSC and SFS Unite

A number of members put forward the idea that the duplication of administration was pointless, and in late March 1925 they persuaded a joint meeting that both clubs should be wound up and their assets handed to a new club to be called the NSW 18-Footer Club. However a number of Flying Squadron members objected to their name disappearing and in May 1925 they rescinded the winding-up motion of the Sydney Flying Squadron but allowed that of the Sydney Sailing Club to continue, so the Sydney Flying Squadron started the 1925-26 season as the sole club catering for the 18-footers, a situation which lasted for the next 10 years. At Mark Foy's suggestion (or perhaps insistence) every second week's race was run in two heats and a final.

Britannia working upwind, 1920's. HALL COLLECTION ANMM

Another newspaper report in December 1924 added more names to the crew list, all Robinsons and all regulars from the beginning. Charlie Robinson was George's cousin and a Soccer coach and official, Les Robinson was George's brother, Syd Robinson was Charlie's brother and had represented Australia and NSW in Soccer and was Captain of the Pyrmont Rangers. The same list had Jack Robinson as for'd hand. This was their brother John, known to the family as Johnny but publicly as Jack. I understand that George still worked for John at the boatyard. It was another mid-field season in earnings (£42), but they managed to gain 2nd place in the State Championship in February 1925. There are more crew lists in Appendix II.

Britannia won a couple of heats early in the 1925-26 season (their seventh) but broke their mast in a squally Westerly in October. They peaked in the middle of the season winning a final in the last race before Christmas in a 50mph Southerly that capsized many boats and caused a lot of damage to others. Then they won the morning race of the Balmain Regatta on New Years Day 1926 and were 2nd in the afternoon race.

Britannia's mast broke for the second time in October 1925.
ONE OF MANY FAMILY PHOTOS DONATED TO THE ANMM BY FAY MAGNER.

Looks like a wet day, *Britannia* under ballooner prior to 1926.
AUSTRALIAN MOTOR BOAT AND YACHTING MONTHLY FEB 1926

The 1926-27 season was not a big one for *Britannia* in terms of wins because there were none, but they managed to get into a lot of places and finish above mid-field in prize money from the SFS and the Balmain Regatta. And at the end of the season, *Britannia* travelled to the Port Macquarie Regatta at Easter for the first time. Several Sydney 18-footers had been going up to this Regatta for a few years now. They travelled up by steamer and were craned into the water at the Port and towed up River to the Regatta grounds by motor boat. This season eight boats went up from Sydney, and in three races, two handicaps and the Hastings River Championship, *Britannia* gained two 4th places (including the Championship race) and took home an additional £14, bringing the season's winnings to £89! They broke their no wins streak the next season when they won a final in March 1928, but it was Jack Robinson at the helm that day. They also capsized once that season (their third) and were third in the State Championship, but the biggest story of that season was the story of the Ratsey and Lapthorne mains'l. Wee Georgie related the story to Bruce Stannard who wrote it up in *Bluewater Bushmen*. George Press always had the best gear for *HC Press (II)* and in

1927 he ordered a new mains'l from the famous Ratsey and Lapthorne loft in Cowes, England. *HC Press* carried it in the Port Jackson Championship on 10 December 1927, and they won. Skipper Chris Webb however was not happy with it, as it appeared to have one tight seam distorting the sail a little. He refused to use it again, allegedly suggesting that it should be turned into a cover. George Press disposed of it to Balmain sailmaker Harry West, and Wee Georgie then bought it for £5. He hung it up, and by careful attachments of weights to points along the seam managed to stretch out the distortion. *Britannia* then carried this sail for quite a few seasons, and beat *HC Press* boat-for-boat a number of times with it.

We were able to confirm this story recently. A colleague, shipwright Simon Sadubin was visiting the Ratsey loft a few years ago while researching the sails for several Fife 6-metre boats he was working on, when he came across an entry for sails for a "Sydney 18' class" for George Press in 1927. So we have the dimensions for that sail, which I used in illustrations of the rig in *The Open Boat*. We were lucky, you can see from the photo that the records were damaged in a fire many years ago. Cheers to Ratsey and Lapthorne for keeping such important records.

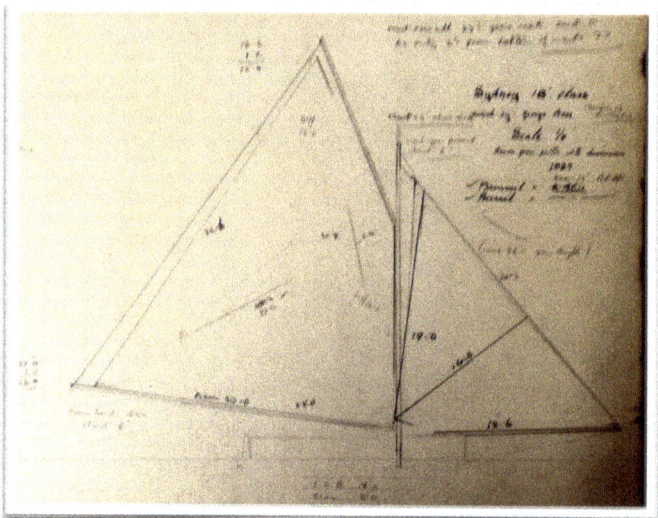

The plan of the Ratsey and Lapthorne sail Wee Georgie bought after being rejected by Chris Webb for George Press's *HC Press*.
SIMON SADUBIN
FROM RATSEY ARCHIVE

Nine boats from Sydney went up to the Port Macquarie Regatta at Easter 1928, and *Britannia* gained a 2nd and a 3rd in handicaps and a 4th in the Hastings River Championship. Brother John left the crew at the end of the season, so another brother Les took over as for'd hand. But another Balmain Tigers footballer Bob Lundie joined the crew at about this time and soon took over setting the extras, and continued as George's for'd hand for 16 seasons, and they remained mates for life.

Britannia crew at Port Macquarie, probably in 1934. With seven annual (Easter) visits between 1927 and 1936 *Britannia* won a lot of prize money, winning the Championship twice.   KEN ROBINSON COLLECTION

1928-29 was a mixed season. There were two capsizes including one which caused some damage to the boat and gear; they won one final and two heats, and gained three 3rds, including in the Port Jackson Championship, and won one of two races at the Balmain Regatta. In three other Championship races Wee Georgie was unlucky. In the SFS Championship in November they lost a man (or two) overboard and lost time picking him (them) up, to finish 9th. In the Bradley's Head Championship in January 1929 *Britannia* didn't finish for an unknown reason, and in the State Championship in February they were leading with only a leg to go when they hit the Shark Island pile and were disqualified. Port Macquarie again worked out successfully when as one of seven boats to travel up, *Britannia* won a handicap and gained second in the Championship to Chris Webb steering *Keriki*.

Webb was steering *Keriki* partly because George Press had withdrawn *HC Press* from racing in the last few races of the season in protest at the long handicaps given to other boats that prevented *HC Press* from winning as often as they would like. They still won the biggest share of prize money, so I can't really be on their side. The dispute was settled before the start of the next season by Press having the handicapper replaced.

Britannia just in front of *Desdemona*.
HARRY THOMPSON COLLECTION SFS

Crew photo late 1920's. Bob Lundie is far left, Charlie Robinson second from left in front, John Robinson third from right in front, Mick Russell far right.
BOB LUNDIE COLLECTION SFS

Chapter 3

Champion!

Britannia missed the first two races of the 1929-30 season due to Wee Georgie's refereeing duties in Rugby League, but he signalled he was back by gaining a 2nd in the first heat on 5 October and a 3rd off 3½ minutes a fortnight later and followed up with a double, winning both heat and final on 26 October. This was definitely a signal that they were going to be competitive that season.

The very next week was the SFS Championship. *Britannia* had a good start in a light northerly and got to the front early and stayed there. Billy Fisher in *Australia* closed to within less than a minute on the third leg, and kept up the pressure but finished 31 seconds behind. Chris Webb in *HC Press* was becalmed at the start but made a great recovery to finish 3rd, two minutes behind. It was a popular win. Wee Georgie was roundly cheered as he came alongside the ferry to pick up the Championship ribbon and was said to be visibly excited. It must have been a great moment for him, after finishing 2nd in eight other Championship races over the 10½ seasons of racing.

A Championship start in the 1920's, *Britannia* second from right.
POSTCARD GRAEME FERGUSON COLLECTION AHSSA

A display of *Britannia's* trophies at George's Little Avenue home in Balmain. The pennants, now all at the ANMM, are from the first few Championships they won. In the centre is the 1929-30 SFS Championship pennant, on the right is the NSW Championship pennant from later that season.
BOB LUNDIE COLLECTION SFS

For the next Saturday's handicap race the handicapper put *Britannia* on scratch, and *HC Press* on half a minute. Webb was so used to having the scratch boat that on the day he refused to take his start and held back until *Britannia* started in the final, and though both boats were unplaced, *Britannia* finished nine seconds ahead after being well behind *HC Press*. The newspapers reported on this contest as much as on the actual winner, and mentioned that when Webb refused to answer his starting flag there was a "loud demonstration" on the ferry. At the weekly meeting of the Squadron Webb was asked to explain himself, and he replied that he would not take a start from anyone. He accused George of having won the Championship by a fluke, and George

HC Press (Chris Webb) leads *Britannia*. Webb and George had some ding-dong battles in the late 20's and early '30's. HARRY THOMPSON COLLECTION SFS

accused Webb of bad sportsmanship, pointing out that he (George) had been runner-up in numerous championship races and may have done even better if he had the money to spend on gear for the boat. Webb refused to take his start on the following Saturday as well, and both boats were unplaced, though Webb finished ahead.

At that week's meeting Webb was told he could be disqualified if he didn't take his start again, but the issue didn't arise on the following Saturday as *HC Press* was placed back on scratch with *Britannia*. There was a bit of argy-bargy, George claimed that Webb forced *Britannia* onto a moored boat off Clark Island, but no umpire witnessed it so nothing could be done.

Crew swinging hard on the run from the Sow and Pigs.
WILLIAM HALL PHOTO IN AUTHOR'S COLLECTION

In the next race both boats were still on scratch, but were both unplaced in their heats, and the final was won by J Courtney in *Australia,* so for the following Saturday *Australia* was placed 15 seconds behind scratch, with *Britannia* and *HC Press* on scratch. *Australia* was effectively giving both boats a start. Webb crossed the line on time to avoid being disqualified, but immediately eased sheets and waited until *Australia* started. All three were unplaced, but *Britannia* finished almost 3½ minutes ahead of *Press*. Newspapers were highly critical of Webb, and the punters particularly were upset. The following week Webb took his start. He won the second race in January 1930 after the Christmas break and for the next few weeks was back on scratch.

On 22nd February *Britannia* proved that her November Championship win was definitely not a fluke by winning the State Championship (*Press* was 14th). The newspapers were full of anticipatory comment and any one of five boats were considered chances: *Australia* under Bill Fisher and occasionally Jack Courtney was the leading prize winner that season and always on or close to scratch, *HC Press* with many championships under the belt, *Britannia* the current SFS Champion, *Arawatta* built and steered by Charlie Hayes, and *Defiance,* last season's State Champion. *Britannia's* recent form was excellent, only disrupted by capsizing the week before the Championship in the Queen of the Harbour race (their second swim that season) after fouling the Shark Island pile again.

In the State Championship in a light Nor'westerly with her big rig with the Ratsey sail *Britannia* got a good start and had hit the lead by Bradley's Head under balloon jib. Positions behind her changed a number of times during the first part of the race with *Australia* threatening at one point, but by the second half of the race *Arawatta* had taken second place, and a ding-dong battle ensued. At one point *Arawatta* got to within a boat length of *Britannia* but on the final work from Shark Island to the finish off Clark Island *Britannia* drew inexorably ahead and beat *Arawatta* over the line by 58 seconds. The elderly *Advance* under George Degan finished 3rd one minute and thirty five seconds later. *Australia* was 10th, *HC Press* was 14th!

We have no photo of **Britannia's** first Championship win in the SFS Championship in November 1929, but we do have this newspaper photo of **Britannia** beating **Arawatta** to take the NSW Championship in February 1930. SYDNEY MORNING HERALD 24 FEB 1930 TROVE NLA

It must have been a wonderful moment for Wee Georgie and his loyal crew, after knocking on the door for so long to win a second Championship in the season. And the total season's prize money of £83 would have helped as well, especially considering they had entered into the start of the Great Depression. Work for George at John's yard would become light on, and George and Kit had a son, Ron born in 1925 and another child on the way, Norma born in 1931.

Britannia finished off the season as usual by going to the Port Macquarie Regatta where they were 2nd in two of the three handicap races. The Championship race was a drifter and was abandoned. Before they left Sydney George had to build a new bumpkin which had carried away in the second last race with Jack Senior at the helm.

A drifter for the Championship race at the Port Macquarie Regatta in 1930. *Keriki* (crescent) is leading, *Britannia* is fourth from right. The race was abandoned. Unfortunately light winds are often experienced on the North Coast of NSW around Easter and affected the Regatta several times. The flag-bedecked starter boat at right is *XLCR*, a trawler with a long history in the Port and which still exists, restored at the local Maritime Museum.

FROM A POSTER PREPARED BY THE RE-ENACTMENT COMMITTEE, 2005. SEE THE YARNS PAGE *THE PORT MACQUARIE REGATTA* AT WWW.OPENBOAT.COM.AU

Chapter 4

Football

Wee Georgie earned his nickname because he was under 5' tall (1.52m) and weighed around 8 stone (50 kg) while playing. According to Rugby League historian David Middleton, Wee Georgie is the smallest first-grade Rugby League player in NSW in the records, out of about ten thousand registered players since 1908.

Starting with the Balmain Arline Junior Rugby League Club in 1912 as a foundation member, George moved to the Balmain President's Cup team (under 21's) in 1914 and later that same year was promoted to Reserve Grade (Second Grade), and in 1915 to First Grade.

George played first-grade for the Balmain Tigers as one of three halfbacks available to the team. The other two were Test players, Arthur "Pony" Halloway and Albert "Rickety" Johnston so George had to be in top form to get a guernsey.

Wee Georgie Robinson in his playing days.
ARROW FRI 3 JUNE 1921
TROVE NLA

George (middle row, fourth from right) was a foundation member of the Balmain Arlines Junior team and he was President in 1919 when this photo of the 3rd-time Premiers was taken, at the same time as he was playing in First Grade and about to launch *Britannia*. KARAS 2009

The Balmain Tigers First Grade Premiership-winning team of 1919. George is second from left at front. CHESTERTON 2000

Balmain was a leading team in the competition, winning Premierships in 1915, 1916, 1917, 1919, 1920 and 1924. George played in four of the Grand Finals, 1915, 1919, 1920 and 1924. He played reserve grade in 1918. He was selected for NSW in 1920 and played against Queensland. From 1920 to 1922 he was selected to represent the Metropolitan team (City) and played a game against New Zealand in 1922. In 1921 just before a First Grade game he heard that he was to be selected for the Kangaroo Tour of Great Britain, but he broke a collarbone in that match and was therefore out of it.

In all between 1915 and 1928 George played 85 First Grade games, winning 51, losing 27 and drawing 7. He scored 24 tries and kicked 44 goals.

As the smallest first-grade player George would have had a tough time of it. David Middleton points out that he played in an era where the game was supervised by only a referee and two touch judges, and the attitude was that what happened on the field stayed on the field. He would have received some protection from his teammates, but still had to be tough. Middleton tells the story that in one game against Eastern Suburbs, two Test forwards Sandy Pearce (also an 18-footer sailor) and Bob "Botsy" Williams were determined to get Wee Georgie and were heard to yell "Kill 'im!" as they both piled on top of him. George had a cut over his right eye, and was taken off and had his wound plastered up and rejoined his team, and got his own back by winning the game.

On 12 July 1924 George was injured in a game, with contusions to the eye and shoulder and was sent to Balmain Hospital. He recovered in time to play in the final on Tuesday 29 July (season shortened due to visit by English team) which Balmain won. At the start of the following season, in April 1925 George announced his retirement from the game. His teammate and crewmate Mick Russell also retired.

In July 1927 the Balmain club announced that they would hold a Testimonial for George, involving an exhibition match and a Dinner/Dance for George, the sixth player to receive this honour which was given to players who had played 12 matches or more in each of 6 consecutive seasons. George would receive the money raised from the match and Dinner with a guaranteed £100. The match took the form of a "Past versus Present" match where the current First Grade team played a team of retired players (who would play half a game each). It was held on Saturday 18 June 1927. In spite of wet weather 1500 people turned up. Past players included George himself as Captain, Chook Fraser, Junka Robinson (no relation) and Pony Halloway. The Present team won 16-12, but George kicked a goal, Chook Fraser scored two tries. Pony Halloway dislocated his shoulder early in the match. The Dance was held after the season on 5 December 1927 at Prescott's Hall Balmain.

George sprints towards the action in the final in 1924. It was the first match ever called on radio. Balmain won 3-0.   CHESTERTON 2000

But after almost three seasons lay-off George had got the taste for the game again and rejoined the First Grade team for the rest of that season. He started the following season in 1928 as Captain of First Grade (with Chook Fraser as coach), but injured his shoulder in July and announced his permanent retirement. But he remained with Balmain Tigers as coach of the President's Cup team and announced he would become a referee. He passed the referee's exam on the first attempt (apparently unusual) and refereed four First Grade games and some minor grades in 1929 but decided that he would rather be a coach.

The players from the "Past and Present" match in June 1927, held as a testimonial to George, who is second row, fourth from left. Others include Chook Fraser back row third from left, Pony Halloway extreme left second back row and Junka Robinson (no relation) extreme left second row. CHESTERTON 2000

He had been nominated for the position of coach of the President's Cup team (under 21's) in 1915 and held the position for a record 39 consecutive years until 1953, coaching them to seven premierships between 1926 and 1952.

George coached the First Grade team for three seasons from 1933 to 1935.

George was the first Life Member of the Balmain Junior League and was also made a life member of the Balmain Football Club and the Balmain Referees Association

A caricature of George at the time of his return to playing after almost three seasons lay-off.
REFEREE 31 AUG 1927 TROVE NLA

Chapter 5

The Great Depression and the Split

At the start of the 1930–31 sailing season Wee Georgie would have been looking forward to getting back into it with *Britannia* as one of the leading boats. He missed the first three races in September and October due to football commitments but started on 18 October in a race with two heats and a final on scratch with *Australia*, but was unplaced in his heat. The following week *Britannia* was disqualified for fouling the Clark Island mark, and the week after that was unplaced again off scratch. After the previous brilliant season this one was turning out very ordinary. The fourth race was the Sydney Flying Squadron Championship and was held in a hard blow in which *Britannia* was over-rigged and forced to lower away in Chowder Bay. Unplaced in the next few races, on 6 December *Britannia* was reported as having collided with a launch at Balmain and did not make the start. But finally on 13 December *Britannia* won the race off ½ a minute and won £15.

Britannia working upwind. HALL COLLECTION ANMM

Britannia missed two seasons, 1931-32 and 1932-33. The fleet sailed on without them as in this shot from the 1931-32 season just prior to the opening of the Sydney Harbour Bridge. HARRY THOMPSON COLLECTION SFS

But bad luck still dogged them in the second half of the season and they did not get into a place in either handicap or Championship events, and *Britannia's* handicap crept out to 3 minutes. They didn't make the usual trip to Port Macquarie at Easter, and at the start of the 1931-32 season Wee Georgie announced that *Britannia* would not be racing this season. He did sail at least once in ten-footers as there is a report of him sailing *Australia* into 3rd place in a Balmain 10' Dinghy Club race on 7 December 1931.

The full story on why *Britannia* did not sail may never be told. But the death of George and Kit's infant daughter Norma in September 1931 would have had an immense effect on their life.

Britannia also stayed out of the 1932-33 season. In February 1933 a newspaper reported that Wee Georgie would take the main sheet on *Tangalooma* a former Queensland Champion now racing on Sydney Harbour and steered by Billy Dunn. I have been unable to determine if this ever happened.

While *Britannia* was not racing a significant development had occurred in 18-footer racing. In September 1932 Brisbane boatbuilder Toby Whereat launched an 18-footer he named *Aberdare* following the "skiff principle" which was only 7 foot in beam with no heel aft (a feature which had been pioneered in the 1920's by Whereat as a builder and Champion sailor of 16-foot skiffs) with a high-peaked battened skiff-type rig. *Aberdare* had absolutely streeted everything in Brisbane in the 1932-33 season and had re-ignited the big-beam boats enthusiasts' fears of the smaller boats in spite of only coming in 3rd in the Australian Championships in January 1933 in Sydney. It had not gone unnoticed that this event was held in a light SE breeze and *Aberdare* did not have a Number One rig so was undercanvassed. A number of members of the Squadron were impressed by the skiff-type boats but there was considerable opposition from the club officials. One described *Aberdare* as "a narrow-gutted mistake". George Press, a long-standing member of the Squadron built a new boat *HC Press IV* in the winter of 1933 with a beam of only 7 foot and along similar skiff-type lines to *Aberdare.* He was begrudgingly allowed to register the boat, and *HC Press IV* began racing with the Squadron on scratch, and won the SFS Championship on 11 November 1933.

A sailor named Bob Cuneo decided to have an *Aberdare* copy built, but knowing that there would be some sort of opposition he kept very quiet about it, and engaged Jack Whereat, father of Toby, to build a boat on the same moulds. Toby unfortunately had died of pneumonia not long after completing *Aberdare,* living just long enough to see that the boat was a resounding success.

Cuneo cheekily named his boat *The Mistake* in reference to the aforementioned criticism, and registered it with the SFS the same night as *HC Press IV*. There was nothing in the rules to prevent the registration, but the Squadron panicked and

The Mistake, a copy of the radical boat *Aberdare* became the focus of the disagreements that split the SFS in 1934-35. TOM CUNEO COLLECTION

Aberdare on one of her first visits to Sydney. After ***Britannia*** retired Wee Georgie steered *Aberdare* for two seasons in the 1940's. SFS COLLECTION

immediately closed the register. *The Mistake* began racing with the Squadron on scratch and stayed on scratch or close to it for the rest of the season.

After the start of the 1933-34 season the *Sydney Morning Herald* announced on 31 October that *Britannia* was to return to racing. They started in the SFS Championship on 11 November in a moderate SE breeze and got into 6th place. The rest of the first half of the season up to Christmas was a washout in terms of placings.

HC Press IV and *The Mistake* remained the scratch boats or close to it for the rest of that season. But the big-beam *Tangalooma* won the State Championship in January (*Britannia* was 6th) and the big-beam *Yendys* won the Bradley's Head Championship in February. But *Aberdare* won the Australian Championship in Brisbane in February 1934.

Britannia won only one race in the rest of that season, a handicap win on 27 January, and her handicap crept out to 4½ minutes. But at Easter she was one of eight

Sydney boats that went up to Port Macquarie and won three out of four races, including the Hastings River Championship and went home with £36!

The 1934-35 season started with five boats on scratch, the two new narrow skiffs *HC Press IV* and *The Mistake* and three older big-beamers *Australia, Yendys* and *Tangalooma. Britannia* was off 2 minutes. The narrow skiffs were quite impressive in their performances but they were not unbeatable. The first Championship race of the season was the SFS Championship in October and it was won by an older boat *Rosetta,* with *Britannia* coming 2nd.

But there was plenty of chatter about the skiff-type boats, and rumours of a breakaway group began to build by December 1934. Then when sailors came back after a brief Christmas and New Year break it was announced that a new club, the NSW 18-Foot Sailing League had been formed with former SFS President James Giltinan as President and with several of the Squadron's fleet as foundation members, including the 1906 *Scot* and *The Mistake*. Giltinan was a sports promoter and had been the force behind the establishment of Rugby League as a breakaway from Rugby Union in 1908. One of his brilliant ideas was to race on Sundays, which meant that a lot of sailors from other classes could sail 18's as well, and track bookmakers would have another outlet. Giltinan cleverly arranged to donate money to charities particularly to the Crippled Children (of which there were many in pre-vaccination days due to the scourge of polio) to appease the wowsers. He also intended that boats could belong to both clubs and race on both days, but the Squadron immediately banned any boats and members that raced with the League. This affected George Press and *HC Press IV* who won the State Championship at the SFS in January but then registered his boat with the League and was expelled from the SFS. Things got quite bitter.

Wee Georgie was nothing if not loyal, being involved with one football club all his life, and stayed loyal to the Squadron. He was actually seriously ill with pneumonia for a period in January and February 1935 and missed a few races but resumed sailing in February and won a couple of handicap races taking his winnings for the season to £63, a not inconsiderable sum seeing the prize money for each win and placing had been reduced for the last few seasons due to the Depression. *Britannia* went to Port Macquarie as usual at Easter and won a handicap, was 2nd in another, and was leading in the Championship race in a drifter when it was called off.

Britannia crew and family picnicking under Bradleys Head waiting for the start of the Anniversary Regatta in January 1934. George is second from right, front row. The boy is son Ron. George's wife Kit holds baby Fay.
BOB LUNDIE COLLECTION SFS

Britannia and crew on the School St slip in mid to late 1930's. Bob Lundie is in front of the mast, and on the seawall is Gordon White, George and Charlie Robinson. Bob joined the crew in the late 1920's and was *Britannia's* forward hand until 1944. George's brother Jack had been in the role from launching until the 1927–28 season. Brother Les took over for a season or so but went back on the jib when Bob Lundie started setting the extras.
BOB LUNDIE COLLECTION SFS

Chapter 6

The Later Years

Without the narrower boats the big-beamers had the racing to themselves on Saturdays, but the fleet had been reduced to between 16 and 19 boats. At the start of the 1935-36 season four boats were on scratch, the 16-year old *Britannia*, the 10-year olds *Yendys* and *Cutty Sark* and the 5-year old *Tangalooma*. *Britannia* was 2nd in the first two races, 2nd in the SFS Championship in November (to *Tangalooma*) and won a handicap race off scratch the following week, in a race which featured a SW squall that resulted in only three boats finishing. But to stop them from getting too cocky they swam off Kirribilli on the way to the start the following week.

In the State Championship in January *Britannia* was again 2nd to *Tangalooma*, with *Yendys* again 3rd, the same placings as in the SFS Championship.

For most of her sailing life **Britannia** was kept in a shed in Snails Bay and paddled around Ballast Point and Simmons Point to the School St yard where she was rigged in the water. In the first shot Albert Robinson (in the bow) and Gordon White (on the thwart) are waiting to receive the mast. KEN ROBINSON COLLECTION

The two 18-footer clubs held alternate Australian Championships. The Queenslanders had also split into two clubs, and four big-beamers came down to Sydney in late January and February but were unplaced in several races held, including the Championship which was won by *Tangalooma*, with *Yendys* 2nd and *Britannia* 3rd. *Tangalooma* won her fourth Championship of the season in the Port Jackson Championship on 15 February 1936 with *Britannia* again 2nd.

The following Saturday the Anniversary Day Regatta was held (it had been cancelled in late January due to the death of the King). The SFS and the League held separate races on the day. *Britannia* was unplaced.

A second capsize for the season in the second last race may have dampened their spirits, but they probably raised them again when in their usual pilgrimage to Port Macquarie at Easter *Britannia* was 4th in a handicap race and won the Hastings River Championship for a second time.

Yendys (red anchor) and ***Britannia*** in one of their many head-to-head battles.
HALL COLLECTION ANMM

Britannia had always had close competition with *Yendys,* with dominance varying between the two. In the 1935-36 season *Britannia* had the edge, but this was reversed in the 1936-37 season. *Yendys* won three Championships, and *Britannia* was only placed in one of them, getting 2nd in the SFS Championship in November. *Yendys* had a real bumper season, winning four handicap races as well for a total of seven wins, a SFS record.

Both boats were sent to Brisbane in late January 1937 for the SFS version of the Australian Championships. They were beaten by *Tangalooma* which had been shipped back to Brisbane and now represented Queensland. *Britannia* was 3rd and *Yendys* unplaced.

Britannia crew on the visit to Brisbane for the Australian Championship in early 1937.
Front row: (from left)"Little Georgie" Robinson, Ron Robinson, George. Les Robinson is in the middle row behind George.
Back row: Jack Halliday (second from left), Bob Lundie (third from left), Mick Russell (third from right), Charlie Robinson (far right). KEN ROBINSON COLLECTION

At Easter 1937 the Port Macquarie Regatta committee did not hold a race for 18-footers, and they made the 16-footer race the main event, and the Regatta ceased to run within a couple of years, being revived briefly after 1947 but still without 18's.

The Squadron fleet numbers were down and so was the number of spectators paying to get on the ferries. A serious bit of re-thinking was taking place at the Squaddie and in 1937 they allowed boats to register which were under the beam restrictions, as well as removing the necessity of having a heel and perhaps more importantly rescinding the motion that had prevented members sailing at both clubs. This allowed George Press to dig the old *HC Press II* out of the shed and race on Saturdays with the SFS while continuing to sail *HC Press IV* at the League on Sundays. A number of other skippers and crew began to sail at both clubs. Several new skiff-type boats joined the SFS at the start of the 1937-38 season including *JL Glick* which was run by the Woolloomooloo Police Boys Club. Several old boats returned from retirement including *Mississippi, Enid* and *Florrie II* which was renamed *Florrie A*. *Cutty Sark* was retired and replaced with *Arawatta,* renamed as *Cutty Sark II*. *Scot* built in 1906 which had left the Squadron to become a foundation member of the League had been sold and renamed *Native* and rejoined the Squadron under George's old crewmate and football teammate Tony Russell. Fleet numbers that season were generally in the low twenties.

The 1937-38 season was a mixed one for *Britannia.* They won four races, including three Championships, the SFS and Port Jackson Championships and the one-off Celebrations Championship for the Sesquicentennial. But they snapped their mast in the Queen of the Harbour race in a 45 mile per hour squall in December. Two weeks earlier George's cousin and long-term mainsheet hand Charlie Robinson's father died (also named Charlie, he had been regular for'd hand for Jack Robinson Snr) and *Britannia* had not raced that Saturday as a mark of respect.

Some of the Squadron fleet in light conditions late 1930's.
JOHN STANLEY COLLECTION

Britannia snapped their mast in a squall in December 1937, the third and last time.
BRIAN GALE SCRAPBOOK

The 1938-39 season was another good one for Wee Georgie and *Britannia*. George was made a Life Member of the Sydney Flying Squadron in October, was mostly on scratch and won five races in the season including the NSW Championship and the Vaucluse Regatta.

The only times *Britannia* was not on scratch that season was when he was pushed out by *Flying Fish,* a heel-less 7-foot beamer built by Norman Wright Sen as *Joyce III* in 1937, and *Narrabeen Lakes,* another skiff-type boat built by Willis Douglass. Douglass had been a 16-foot skiff builder until the League was established after which he became Sydney's most prolific 18-foot skiff builder.

At some stage in 1939 Wee Georgie started to work as a shipwright on Cockatoo Island, the naval base that was expanding due to the War.

The following season was not as successful. *Britannia* had no wins at all that season and had a few DNF's due to gear failure and some others due to being overcanvassed. The handicap crept out to 2, but they did get fastest time at least once. Their best results were a 2nd in a handicap and 3rd places in both the State Championship and the Port Jackson Championship, the winner of the latter being *Native,* the former *Scot* of 1906 which had won *Britannia's* first race in 1919!

Native under Tony Russell continued this line of success into the 1940-41 season, including placings in Championships and often getting fastest times in handicap events. *Britannia* won only one handicap race and her handicap went out to 3 minutes at one stage. The biggest prize winner that season was *Top Dog II,* which was the re-named 1938 Wright boat *Taree* which had won the World Championship organised by the League in 1938. You can read the whole story in Robin Elliott's *Galloping Ghosts* (see Bibliography).

A sequence of shots, late 1930's.

BOB LUNDIE COLLECTION SFS

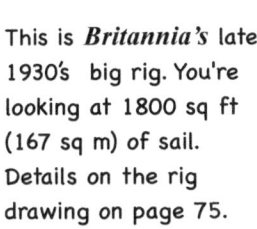

This is *Britannia's* late 1930's big rig. You're looking at 1800 sq ft (167 sq m) of sail. Details on the rig drawing on page 75.

Crew photo from the early 1940's at George's Little Avenue home. <u>Back row</u>: the four at left are unknown, then Gordon White and Charlie Robinson. <u>Middle row</u>: Jack Halliday left then Les Robinson. <u>At front:</u> George, Ron Robinson, Albert "Fatty" Robinson.
BOB LUNDIE COLLECTION SFS

In spite of the War, the Squadron had 26 boats on the register in the 1940-41 season, but this reduced to 22 boats for the 1941-42 season. *Britannia* opened the season with a bang by winning the first race off half a minute and recording fastest time. But they failed to finish the next two races, one because it was blowing too hard for the rig chosen, and the other because it was blowing too light and only six boats finished within the time limit.

A hard Nor'easter on 29 November gave the opportunity for a couple of classic photographs included here. It blew 45 knots, and from a fleet of 18 starters only seven boats finished. *Britannia* was 4th off 1½ minutes. There were only two more races sailed on the main part of the Harbour after this. The Japanese attacks on Pearl Harbour and Malaya led to the closing down of the Harbour to pleasure craft, and the last race of the year was held on 20 December on the upriver Number One course, starting and finishing in Snails Bay. *Britannia* completed the second half of the season with a few more placings including 2nd place in the Port Jackson Championship in February 1942, and getting another fastest time in the last race at the end of March. *Britannia's* £36/4/- prize money for the season was awarded in War Savings Certificates.

Two great mates, George and Bob Lundie at the Little Ave house in the early 1940's same day as the previous photo. The Harbour is just over the fence to the left. The shed in the background is White's Engineering, with lighters with derricks moored alongside.
BOB LUNDIE COLLECTION SFS

Britannia bursts through a wave during a gale on 29 November 1941.
BRIAN GALE SCRAPBOOK, FROM SUNDAY TELEGRAPH 30 NOV 1941

Britannia is just in front of ***Zephyr*** in the gale of 29 Nov 1941.
BOB LUNDIE COLLECTION SFS, ALSO REPRODUCED IN SUNDAY TELEGRAPH 30 NOV 1941

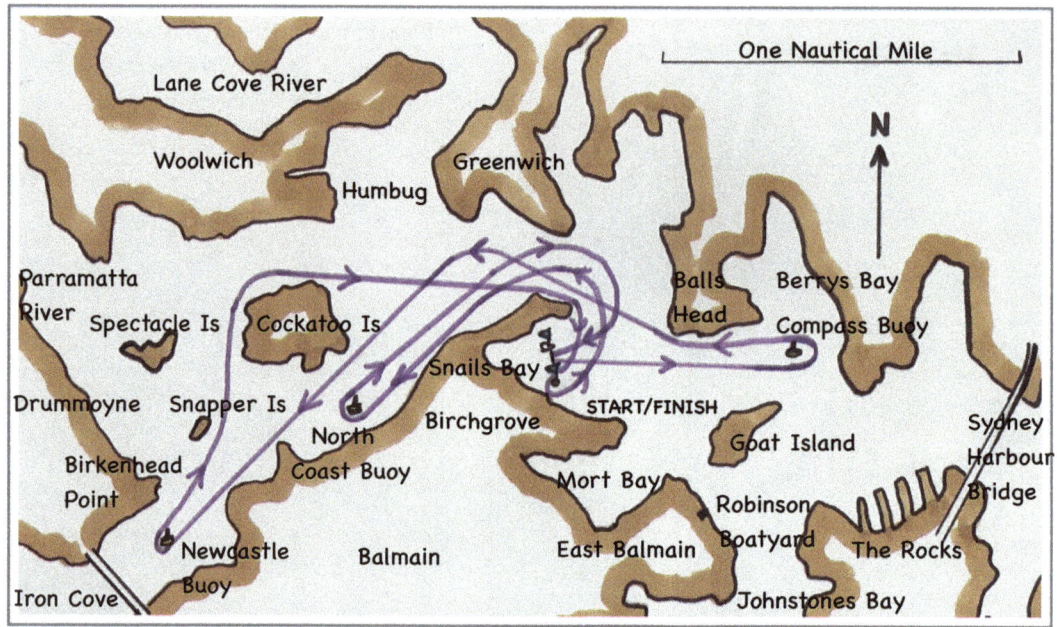

The Number One upriver course 1942-1945. There were a few other courses over the period but this was the one most used. Starting in Snails Bay they went to the Compass Buoy at the mouth of Berrys Bay, then to the Newcastle Buoy off Birkenhead Point, around Cockatoo and back to Snails Bay, to the North Coast Buoy off the coal loader and back to the finish in Snails Bay. The SFS raced on Saturdays, the League raced somewhat similar course on Sundays. Weekend shifts were popular for workers at the Cockatoo Island dockyard because they could watch the races.

The 1942-43 season fleet was rarely more than 10 boats. At least one ferry still followed the fleet. Brian Gale from the well-known sailing Gale family, who was one of the leading for'd hands in 18's in the late 1930's had joined the Air Force but was on leave in Sydney and on the ferry on 28 November when *Desdemona* hailed the ferry and asked if there were any experienced sailors aboard who could join them. Brian stripped off his uniform and dived in and swam to the boat.

Britannia won three handicap races that season and was 2nd again in the Port Jackson Championship (to *Native* again, the former *Scot* of 1906). The Galloping Ghost *Aberdare* joined the Squadron fleet after an absence from sailing of a couple of years, now steered by Bert Swinbourne who was banned from sailing with the League for not returning the World Championship trophy he won in 1938 but lost in controversial circumstances in New Zealand in 1939 (you can read the whole story in Elliott's *Galloping Ghosts,* see Bibliography). *Aberdare* won the SFS Championship and a number of handicap races that season and was almost always on scratch. This season also saw the first appearance at the tiller of Wee Georgie's son Ron, who steered on 3 April aged 16, but was unplaced.

Britannia works upwind in Snails bay where the War years races started and finished. Ron Robinson regularly sailed at this time and is likely aboard in the photo. When researching the boat before building the replica I asked Ron if he remembered how the name was painted on the stern, as this was the only photo I have seen of the stern and there is no signwriting. Ron said that at some stage in the 1930's an out-of-control spinnaker pole went straight through the tuck, and when it was repaired the name was not painted back on. AUTHOR'S COLLECTION

Britannia racing up the Parramatta River during the War years.
HALL COLLECTION ANMM

Britannia won the second race of the 1943-44 season in a light breeze with her big gear, and was leading in another light race in heavy rain in late November when the race was called off after three hours. On 13 November *Britannia* won the SFS Championship which is commemorated in the poster pictured.

On Thursday 20 January George's stepmother Elizabeth (Jack's wife) was one of 16 people killed when the Kempsey Mail train smashed into a local bus at the Brooklyn level crossing in one of Sydney's worst train disasters. *Britannia* did not compete the following Saturday.

They won their last Championship on 19 February 1944 in the Port Jackson Championship. George's nephew Ken Robinson remembers as a boy being invited off the ferry to sail back to the shed on the boat. Two weeks later Ron Robinson at the age of 18 steered the boat into 2nd place in a handicap race off 2 minutes (to *Native* again, off scratch). They finished off the season with a disqualification, two 3rds, and in the final race were last of nine boats after losing their jib in a squall.

In September 1944 Wee Georgie announced *Britannia's* retirement from racing.

A poster made to commemorate *Britannia's* win in the SFS Championship in November 1943, her 13th and second-last Championship win. AUTHOR'S COLLECTION

Chapter 7

The Post War Years

There are several references in newspaper columns regarding the possibility of George building a modern-type 18-footer for himself, but nothing happened along these lines for a few seasons. George had most of the 1944-45 season off, but made at least one guest appearance when he steered *HC Press VII* into 2nd place in a handicap race in January 1945.

For the 1945-46 season George was engaged by Bill Anderson, a club official and generous multiple boat owner to sail *Aberdare* which had not sailed for a season and a bit. Unplaced in the first two races of the season, George then opened a record-breaking patch of form by winning a handicap off scratch on 6 October, a 2nd and a 3rd in the next two races, then three wins in a row including the SFS Championship. His father Jack, then 90, presented George with the ribbon. The core of his *Britannia* crew had stayed with him, cousin Charlie on sheet, second cousin Albert, Herb Robson, G.Davis, H.Mathews and of course Bob Lundie for'd. Son Ron was not in the crew that day as he had just had an appendix operation.

The *Aberdare* crew. From left possibly Eddie Isberg, Bob Lundie, George Davis, Herb Robson, Charlie Robinson, Wee Georgie, Albert Robinson, Ron Isberg.
BOB LUNDIE COLLECTION SFS

Dorothy Fisk chats with George on a very light Queen of the Harbour day in February 1946.

THE SUN, 10 FEB 1946 TROVE NLA

The fleet moved back to the Harbour on 8 December 1945 and it was a gala day, George winning in *Aberdare* in front of 800 people on the ferry and 5000 on shore, in a race they called the 55th Club Championship (somehow separate from the Sydney Flying Squadron Championship earlier that season). For some reason they raced back upriver for the next few weeks, but were back on the Harbour for the State Championship on 12 January which *Aberdare* also won. Fleets were down to about 9 or 10 boats which certainly made it easier to win, but *Aberdare's* performance that season broke a number of records.

Aberdare won a total of 8 races that season and many places. A shadow was cast however when in a combined race with the League on 8 December no SFS boats were in the first seven places! And a personal shadow occurred when father Jack Robinson died in March 1946.

George's second season on *Aberdare* got underway reasonably well with George registering fastest times for three races in a row, but only two wins in handicaps before winning the SFS Championship on 16 November 1946, followed by a win in the 56th Club Championship a month later. *Aberdare* was selected as one of four boats to contest the Australian Championships in Sydney in January 1947, the first time the SFS had conducted an interstate for ten years. The three Queensland boats completely dominated the series, held in three heats. The best *Aberdare* could do was a 4th in one heat. The six-foot beamers were the way to go. *Aberdare* won a couple more Club handicaps, but George had seen the writing on the wall and didn't sail *Aberdare* for a third season.

In the winter of 1947 George and Ron built a six-foot beam 18 they named *Scamp*, using the 6-pointed red star of Jack Robinson's *Livonia* as the insignia. Ron skippered, Wee Georgie occasionally appeared on the mainsheet. *Scamp's* first win was halfway through the first season in January in the Queen of the Harbour race, with Ron's sister Fay aboard. Wee Georgie skippered the boat on at least one occasion, when Ron was on his honeymoon.

The launch of *Scamp*, a 6'-beam 18-footer built by Ron and George Robinson in 1947. Ron's wife Beryl has the champagne, George is second from left, Happy Harry Thompson on far right, not looking his usual happy self.
SFS COLLECTION

Ron Robinson sailed *Scamp* until 1951. He used *Livonia's* 6-pointed red star as his sail logo.
KEN ROBINSON COLLECTION

Ron sailed *Scamp* for four seasons and though they never won a Championship race they were often well up there in Championships and won a fair share of handicap races. Ron skippered *Sylvia Too* owned by the Woolloomooloo Police Boys Club in the 1951-52 and 1952-53 seasons. In 1954 he built *Scamp II*, but very quickly changed the name to *Ampol* as sponsorship had arrived in the 18-footer fleet. He campaigned a series of *Ampols I-IV* until 1965, the highlight being gaining 2nd in the World Championship (JJ Giltinan series) in the 1963-64 season. Ron's cousin Ken who sailed with him relates that they would have won but capsized in the last heat when they selected too big a spinnaker.

Ampol, the third boat of four of that name built and campaigned by Ron Robinson. They were runner-up in the World Championship of 1963-64 season. KEN ROBINSON COLLECTION

Ron joined the Australian Historical Sailing Skiff Association (see Chapter 8) in the early 2000's and though in his eighties he built and sailed a ten-footer he also named *Scamp,* again displaying the 6-pointed red star as insignia. His sons Alan and Barry sailed with him and carried on with *Scamp II* after Ron retired due to illness, before passing away in 2015.

Ron Robinson, 1990's.
ROBINSON FAMILY PHOTO

Other sailing Robinsons

Ken, son of George's brother Les, sailed in the *Ampols* with Ron for many seasons in the late 1950's and early 1960's. Like most of the Robinsons Ken was a shipwright and built his own 18-footer he named *Brooklyn* after the Hawkesbury River town he was from (Les had built a house next to father Jack in Brooklyn and travelled by train, an hour's journey each way to sail on *Britannia*), in January 1949 and campaigned it at the SFS for the rest of that season, the whole of the 1949-50 season and half of the 1950-51 season.

***Brooklyn*, built and campaigned by Ken Robinson over three seasons.** KEN ROBINSON COLLECTION

Vic Robinson was the son of John (Jack Jnr) and had a long career in 18-footers sailing boats such as *Ardath, Aberdare* (the original, still sailing in the early 1950's), *Argus, Fidget* and *The Fox*.

The Fox, one of many boats sailed by Vic Robinson in the 1950's and '60's. *The Fox* also carried Vic's grandfather's 6-pointed red star.
JOHN STANLEY COLLECTION

Britannia Becomes a Motor Boat

Britannia remained in the shed in Snails Bay but at some stage in the late 1940's George decided to turn her into a motor boat. He removed the fin case and installed an engine, added a deadwood to take the shaft, and fitted a coachhouse. Very little else was changed, the three thwarts remained, the round-fronted coaming became the base line for the new cabin and the decks remained the same.

Britannia was converted to a motor launch.
BOB LUNDIE COLLECTION SFS

George was still the Sydney Flying Squadron starter in 1972 when this shot of several legends of the sport was taken at the Presentation Night in June. George is standing, the others are from left Alan Cole, President of the 18-Footer Sailing League, Alf Beashel Secretary of the League, Bob Lundie President of the SFS and Olympian Bill Northam Patron of the SFS. Historically this was a relatively rare moment of cooperation between the two clubs. BOB LUNDIE COLLECTION SFS

In the early 1950's George volunteered to take on the role of starter for the SFS, using *Britannia* as the starter boat, on a temporary basis until they could find someone else. He said that it remained temporary for the next 28 years.

Britannia herself wasn't the starter boat for all that time. In 1964 George built a 19' clinker launch, in the side yard at Elliott St Balmain where he and his wife Katherine lived in an extension he had built to his daughter Fay's house (now Fay Magner). He named it *Brit,* and it remained the starter boat until George retired after 28 years in the role.

The clinker-built ***Brit*** in SFS starter's role off Clark Island in March 1973. ROBINSON FAMILY COLLECTION

Towing ***Ampol*** back to Balmain after a race, 1960's.
ROBINSON FAMILY COLLECTION

Brit is still going strong in 2020 having had a succession of dedicated owners.
GRAHAM PROCTOR

As well as starting the 18's, *Britannia* and then *Brit* also acted as the starting boat for the Snails Bay Sabot Sailing Club which was a Junior club that George had a dominant hand in setting up. The first race was on 4 February 1962 with a fleet of eight Sabots. George had built at least three of them. Ron was generally the starter, George was the Vice-Commodore and Coach and his grandchildren Alan and Barry (Ron's sons) and Rhonda (Fay's daughter) were competitors. Boatbuilder Nick Masterman joined in the second season. Most of the kids involved lived within walking distance.

Their clubhouse was the boatshed at 103 Louisa Road belonging to Stan Nicholson of Nicholson ferries. In 1969 Stan died and the Club moved along to Dodd's shed where *Britannia* had been stored for many years, but room was restricted. In 1973 the Club moved over and formed Drummoyne Sailing Club's Junior division. The whole story is excellently told in Asa Wahlquist's book *Snails Bay Sabot Sailing Club* (see Bibliography). The life span of the club in Snails Bay was during a time of great change in Balmain with maritime industry starting to move out or close down, and increasing gentrification. It was the last hurrah of the old waterfront Balmain.

Britannia was the starter boat for the Snails Bay Sabot Sailing Club in the 1960's, a club that trained many young Balmain sailors including Wee Georgie's grandchildren. GIL WAHLQUIST.

Chapter 8

Restoration and Revival

In 1981 journalist Bruce Stannard published *Bluewater Bushmen* which included a large collection of photographs from William Hall Senior and Junior of the open boats of the Harbour from the 1880's to the 1940's. It was a seminal work, for many people including myself it was an introduction to this fascinating world of open boat racing. Bruce had grown up next to the boatshed at School St Balmain where *Britannia* had been built, and spent a lot of time with Wee Georgie in the late 1970's recording his memories. Wee Georgie's stories are a large part of *Bluewater Bushmen*. Boating writer Jeff Toghill followed this up with another book of Hall photos *Sydney Harbour of Yesteryear* in 1982 which included some of the images of open boats as well as a number of images of yachts.

Bruce Stannard had also been appointed in the late 1980's to the board of the new Australian National Maritime Museum that was being set up with a huge new building under construction in Darling Harbour. Bruce was rightly convinced that such a Museum would need to have an 18-footer in its collection. During the 1980's Wee Georgie had been restoring *Britannia* to the point where he had removed the engine, shaft and deadwood as well as the cabin, and had replaced the fin case. His expressed intention was to donate it to the Sydney Heritage Fleet, a volunteer group that had coalesced around the restoration of the *Lady Hopetoun* steamship and the *James Craig* square-rigger. George Robinson died in 1987 before he could complete the restoration. He left the boat to his old for'd hand Bob Lundie. Bob was a canny chap who knew the nation should pay something for such a significant boat and Bruce Stannard was able to convince the ANMM board to meet Bob's price, and *Britannia* was purchased as the first acquisition of the new Australian National Maritime Museum.

George began restoring *Britannia* into its sailing configuration in the 1980's. DAVID LIDDLE

Arthur Griffith, a friend of Wee Georgie's who was an experienced boatbuilder though a pattern-maker by trade had assisted Georgie in the early stages of restoration and was engaged by the Museum to restore *Britannia* in his shed on the South side of Snails Bay. Arthur however passed away after a short time on the boat, and in 1990 shipwrights Rick Wood and Nigel Shannon were engaged to complete the restoration under the supervision of Michael Staples a shipwright and Conservator at the Museum and Daina Fletcher a Museum Curator. Naval architect Alan Payne and his nephew David Payne were engaged to take the lines off the hull and draw up plans that the team could work off. David is now Curator of the Australian Register of Historic Vessels at the Museum.

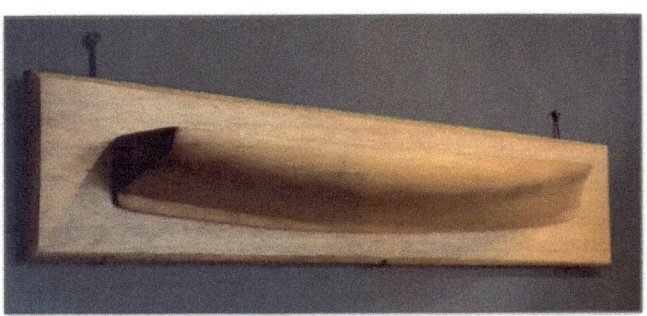

The original half-hull model of *Britannia*, donated to the Australian National Maritime Museum by the family.

FROM THE VIDEO "*CENTENARY OF 18-FOOTER BRITANNIA*", IAN SMITH BOATS CHANNEL, YOUTUBE

The partially-restored *Britannia* being taken to the Museum.
BOB LUNDIE COLLECTION SFS

The Museum made the decision that the boat would not be restored for sailing, but would be made solid enough for display but retaining as much of the original fabric as possible. This approach preserves as much as possible of what Wee Georgie placed there, as a reference for future study. This attracted some criticism from some boatbuilders who felt it should have been restored for sailing even if that meant almost all of the wood was replaced. Personally I think the Museum made the right decision for reasons I will go into later. People who knew the boat such as Bob Lundie and Ron Robinson were extensively consulted and a lot of memorabilia was donated to the Museum by members of the family, including the original half-model on which the hull was based.

Britannia was on display in the main hall of the ANMM from 1990 to 2016. ANMM

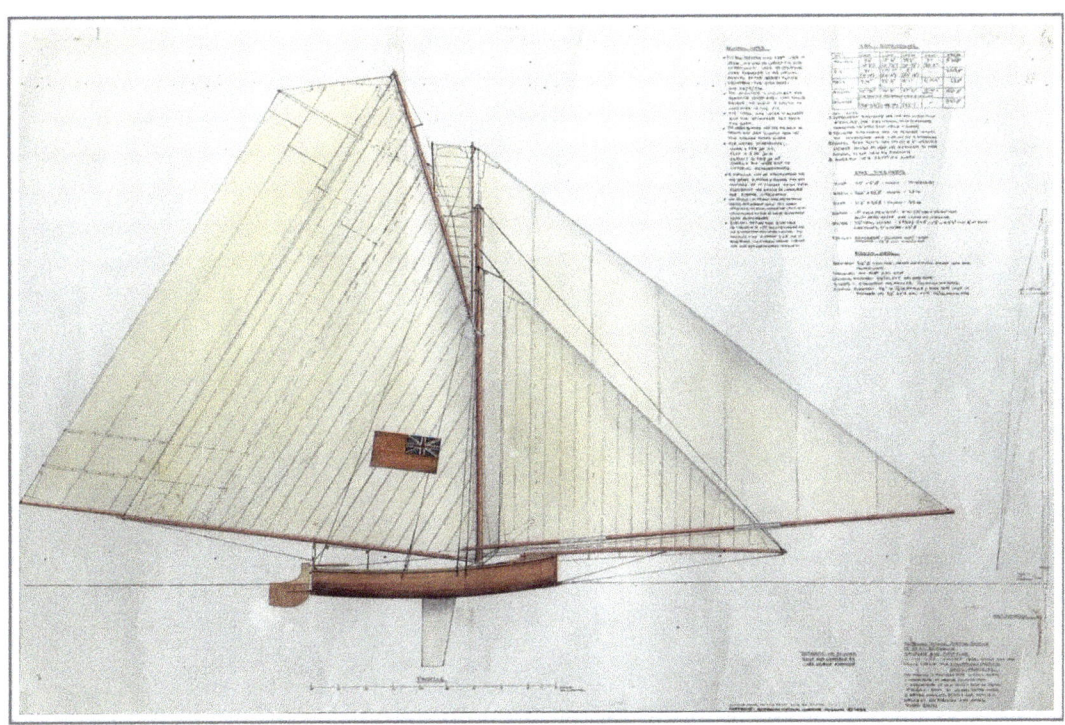
David Payne's drawing of the Number One rig for the ANMM. AUTHOR'S COLLECTION

Britannia received a new rig based on David Payne's research based on known dimensions published in 1937. Michael Staples built the spars and Dennis McGoogan who had apprenticed with Harry West and was one of the last sailmakers alive to have experience of making cotton sails was given the task of making two complete sets of big rig sails in cotton. The boat was made strong enough to suspend from the rafters of the new building, and was on display from the Museum's opening in 1990. Except for a brief interlude in 2001 when bigger boats around it had to be moved, *Britannia* remained on display until 2016.

Painting by Ross Shardlow used on Australia Post stamp, 1992.

With the Centenary coming up in 2019 I was able to convince the Museum to put *Britannia* back on display and I and the crew of the replica assisted Museum staff to raise the rig. *Britannia* is now on display again in the foyer of Wharf 7 adjacent to the main Museum building in Darling Harbour.

The crew of the replica assisted Museum staff to rig ***Britannia*** for display in September 2019 in the foyer of the Wharf Seven building. You can see the Sydney Heritage Fleet's restored ***Yendys*** (red anchor) in the background. PHIL MOORE

The Australian Historical Sailing Skiff Association

In 1989 champion 18-footer sailor of the 1970's Robert Tearne had the idea of setting up an organisation to support building and sailing replicas of Australian open boats. He got together with a number of other retired 18-footer sailors including Graeme Ferguson and World Champion Len Heffernan and other interested parties and formed the Australian Historical Sailing Skiff Association (AHSSA) in 1990. Robert had spent some time talking to Wee Georgie in the 1980's and had a friend Campbell Wallace take the lines of the original model of Wee Georgie's 6-footer *Britannia*. George advised Robert that if he was to build a 6-footer for himself he needed it to be deeper and more substantial that the *Britannia* as George had built it for himself when he weighed under 50 kilograms. So Robert built a 6-footer he called *Wee Georgie* using fibreglass over a simple mould, rigged it and began to sail it and learn how to handle it.

Robert soon decided that 10-footers would be a more suitable class to replicate, and built a batten-seamed cedar planked 10-footer he named *Janis*. He began to sail this with other members of the AHSSA. Another member Reg Barrington began to build another 10-footer based on the lines of a 1940's 12-footer named *Dove*, with the assistance of Len Heffernan. Reg and Len went on to build a series of 10-footers and they began to race regularly. In 1990 Robert Tearne and Graeme Ferguson built a replica of the 10-footer *Commonwealth* from accurate lines taken off the original model by Norman Wright Junior, son of the original builder.

In 1994 Reg Barrington, again with the assistance of Len Heffernan built a replica of the 18-footer *Tangalooma* of 1930, from the original lines plan which still exists. No sooner had *Tangalooma* started sailing than Reg started another, a replica of *Scot* of 1906 using lines taken off a model which we now believe to be of doubtful accuracy.

Robert Tearne founded the Australian Historical Sailing Association and began to build replicas of Aussie open boats, and sail them hard. This is *Janis*, the first 10-footer replica.
JOHN FREDERICKSON

Robert Tearne and Graeme Ferguson's *Commonwealth*, modelled on a Norman Wright 10-footer from 1906.
PHOTOGRAPHER UNKNOWN

Both these 18-footer replicas and all of the boats built by Reg and Len and later builders had hulls that were laminated rather than planked with battened seams. Other than *Janis* and *Commonwealth* all of the other 10-footers were based on 1940's 12-footers and had 1940's-style high-peaked skiff rigs, which undoubtedly made them faster than the original two traditional replicas, but I personally think we lost something by not retaining the batten-seam planked hulls and the more traditional rigs.

It was about this time that yours truly got involved. I was never a skiff sailor, I had mostly sailed yachts but having known Robert Tearne and some of the others through boatbuilding I was invited to crew on *Janis* one day in the Summer of 1993-94 in a race out of Drummoyne Sailing Club with a fleet of I think four or five replica 10-footers. Even though we capsized on the second lap around Cockatoo Island the first part was some of the most enjoyable sailing I'd ever done! I decided on the spot to build one.

Following Robert Tearne's lead I built a 6-footer first, named it *The Balmain Bug* and began to sail it. It was a steep learning curve. I strip-planked the 6-footer, but then I began to build a traditionally planked 10-footer based on the lines of a 1900 10-footer called *Viola* taken off the original model still in the hands of the Dempsey family, the original owners. I began to sail this boat I named *Republic* with the 10-footer fleet that was now competing about once a month, and to sail on either *Tangalooma* or the *Scot* which were now racing several times a season. I resolved to build an 18-footer as soon as I could. Very early on I decided it would be a replica of *Britannia* for two main reasons: the significance of *Britannia* in the history of open boat sailing and of the Sydney Flying Squadron, and the important fact that the boat still existed and could be replicated with a great degree of accuracy.

The first moulds are set up on the keel of the replica in 2001.
FROM THE VIDEO *"BUILDING BRITANNIA"*, IAN SMITH BOATS CHANNEL, YOUTUBE

Nearing completion in 2002. The replica was built in the old Halvorsen boatbuilding shed in Putney.
BOB CHAPMAN

The building process has been thoroughly covered in my 2017 book *The Open Boat* (see Bibliography) and the video *Building Britannia*. I was able to replicate every detail, including the planking line-out (to within about 10mm) and used the same timber species in every case except for the bottom stringers which are of Silver Ash because no suitable NZ Kauri could be found. If Wee Georgie was able to be plonked down at the tiller he would say "There's something different about it, but I can't put my finger on it...". We do use terylene sails and ropes rather than natural fibres. I had to draw the line somewhere. Not only is good cotton sailcloth difficult to find, I didn't want to spend every Sunday drying sails.

The original ......

.....and the replica

IAN SMITH

The *Britannia* replica sails every Summer Saturday with the Sydney Flying Squadron fleet of historical 18-footer replicas. BRUCE KERRIDGE

The *Britannia* replica was launched on 19 October 2002 by Fay Magner, Wee Georgie's daughter, and has raced with the historical 18 footer replica fleet at the Sydney Flying Squadron every Summer Saturday since then. There have been 11 replicas of boats from the period 1906 to 1950 built in Sydney, and one in Brisbane.

As of the 2019-20 season eight boats regularly turn up to sail. The fleet is a familiar sight to anyone who regularly sails on Sydney Harbour. The Sydney Flying Squadron engages a ferry (always a traditional wooden Rosman ferry) to follow the fleet and it is one of the best days out you can have on "Our Beautiful".

With the original boat preserved and on display at the Australian National Maritime Museum and the replica regularly racing on the Harbour, Michael Staples who had a lot to do with the restoration has pointed out that we have the best of both worlds. A historical boat as an artefact is only half the story, the other half being how it behaves in the water. We now have the original boat with much of the timber Wee Georgie Robinson put in place, and a replica which we can sail hard and learn from. If my replica is damaged or lost, it will be a blow to me personally and for a number of people involved, but if *Britannia* had been rebuilt to sailing condition and damaged or lost it would be a blow to the nation and our maritime heritage. With the original preserved, if in another hundred years someone wants to build another replica, the information is all there within Wee Georgie's structure.

Above: The original *Britannia*, early 1920's. HALL COLLECTION
Below: The replica *Britannia*, early 2000's. DAVID TETLEY

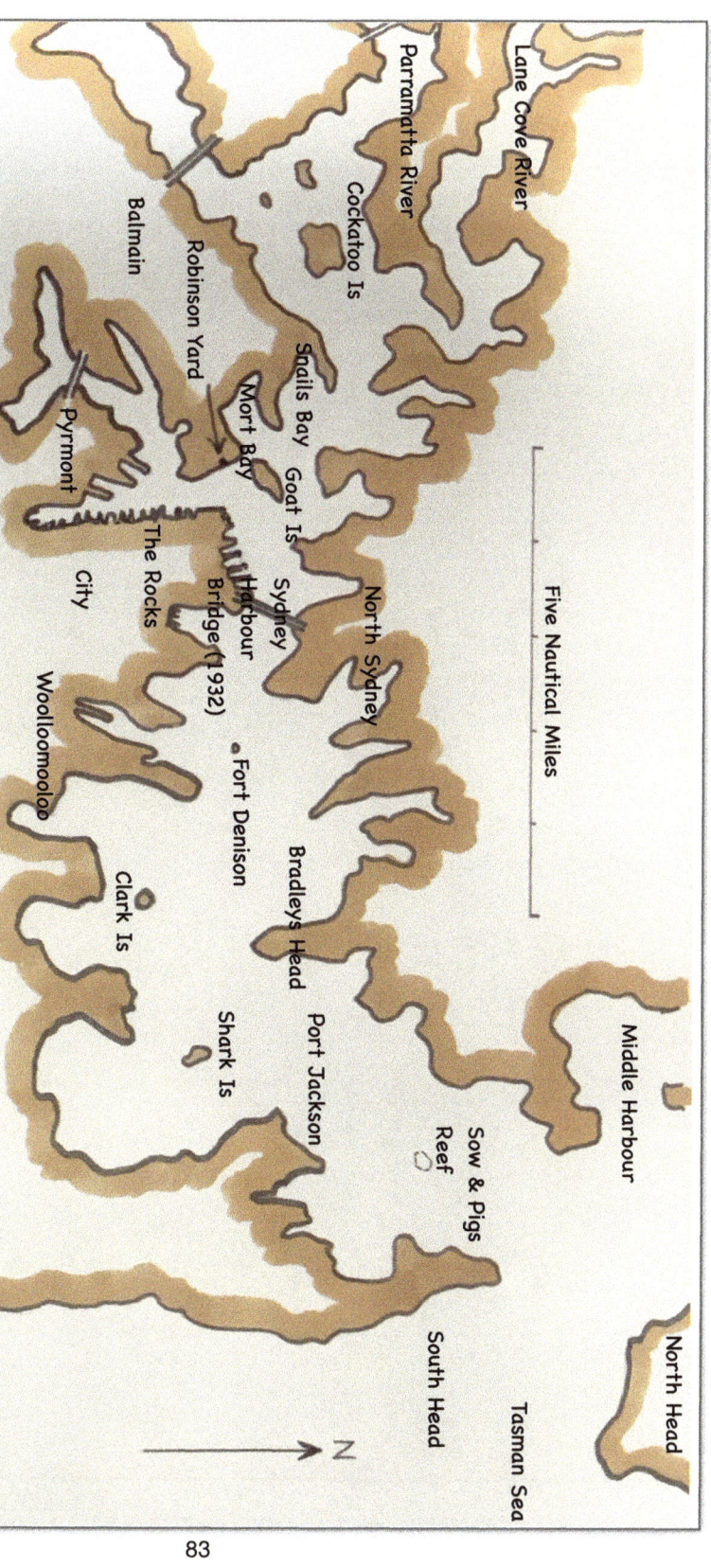

Sydney Harbour is a ria, a drowned river valley. The area of the map is entirely urban, except for some headlands which were retained for military purposes and are now parks. Tidal range is max 2m (6'), currents rarely more than 1½ knots. Prevailing Summer sea breeze is from the North-East (about 55% of Summer afternoons), varies from 12-25 knots and occasionally more, averages 15-20 knots. Southerlies (generally fresh) and South-Easterlies are next most common. Winds from North-West to South-West are relatively uncommon in Summer, and generally hot and unstable when they do blow.

The Sydney Flying Squadron had no premises of its own until the mid-1950's. Boats were stored in boatsheds all around the Harbour (*Britannia* was kept in a shed at Snails Bay) and met at Clark Island for the start.

Appendix I

Boats built by John Robinson Jnr and Wee Georgie Robinson*

John Robinson (1887-1957), George's older brother built a few boats from at least as early as 1906, but we cannot determine where. He served as an officer in the Australian Flying Corps in Britain during the First World War and on his return in 1919 he set up as a boatbuilder in leased premises at 8 School St East Balmain, (the house still exists, technically now 7 Gallimore Ave). He remained in business there until 1953. The yard slipped and maintained boats as well as building new boats to order. In the earlier years George and father John Senior worked at the yard when work was available. George worked

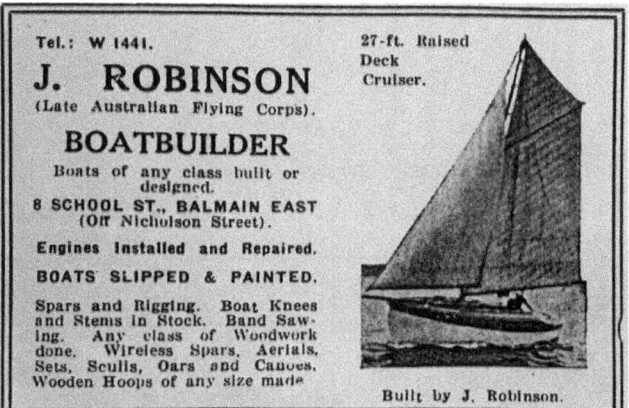

An advertisement in Australian Motor Boat and Yachting Monthly Aug 1926

there most of the time from 1919 to about 1930 when the Depression hit. He also worked there most of the time in the 1930's, up until 1939 when he went to Cockatoo Island and stayed there until he retired in 1959. John Senior bought property in Brooklyn North of Sydney in the 1920's and built a house and commercial boatshed which he ran until his death in 1946 aged 90.

John Robinson and his English war bride Ella on the verandah of their house in School St Balmain just above the workshop and slipway.
SUNDAY TIMES 7 DEC 1919

* Compiled with assistance from Simon Sadubin and Mori Flapan
www.boatregister.net

List of known boats built:

1906   *Young Jack* 18-footer for his father.

1907   *Zanita* (pictured p87) 18-footer for W Martin.

1908   *Livonia* (pictured p9) 18-footer with and for Jack Senior.

1913   *Istria* 30.6' x 8.6' canoe-sterner yawl for Mr Barker. Possibly was the *Istria* lost with all hands off Fraser Island Qld in 1972.

1915   *Britannia* (pictured p10) 6-footer designed and built chiefly by George.

1918   *Iona* 6-footer.

1919   *Weve* motor launch for Mr French.

1919   *Britannia* 18-footer, designed and built chiefly by George. I'm sure both Jack and John assisted as the boat was said to have been built in 6 weeks. On display at Australian National Maritime Museum.

1922   *Waitangi* (pictured p89), 30' yacht for HL Carter.

1922   *Endeavour* 40' yawl, not a definite Robinson boat.

1924?   *Schemer* 12' skiff, four times Champion of Australia.

1925   Cruiser for Mr Fisher

1926   *Cynisca,* (pictured on Boatbuilders advertisement on page 83) 27' Prince-class yacht for FSJ Young.

1927   Raised deck cruiser 28' to WD Bailey's Dolphin design for L Perks.

1927   Cutter 30'x10' for Mr Holohan.

1927   Speedboat 20' for Mr Antin.

1928   *Faerie* 27.3'x8.5' coachhouse yacht to WD Bailey's *Albatross* design for Dr S Hughes. Restored and afloat on Pittwater, Sydney. John Robinson may have also built a raised-deck version. Plans pictured p87.

1928   Double-ended coachhouse yacht, 28' for Mr Barnes.

1928   Motor Cruiser 30'x10' for J Dixon.

1929   *Lady Clara,* 28'x9' yacht for Mr Clarke.

1929   Speedboat 18', similar to Chriscraft for Mr Camphin.

1929   Auxiliary cruiser 28'x9' for Mr McPherson.

1929   Cruiser 32'x10'3" for Mr Audsley.

1930   Boat for Mr Whiteman.

1930   10-footer *Jean* for Mr McFarlane (George), pictured p87.

1930   *Coranto* 30'x8' yacht. Restored c2000, still in Queensland.

1930's George was engaged by the owner of the 10-footer *Commonwealth* built by Norman Wright in Brisbane in 1906 to build a new 10-footer which would have been *Commonwealth II*. The project only got as far as a half-hull model which the family still retains. The author took the lines off the model some time ago and if I build another 10-footer that will be it.

1933   Reported building a 33' x 10' cruiser.

1933   *Hoona* bridge deck cruiser for V Heine. This may be the same boat as the previous entry.

1934   Cruiser 30'x10'6" for FA Homer.

1934   *Swerdna* two different boats recorded of same name, 40'2" and 34' for JO Andrews. Became Naval Auxiliary patrol boat in 1941.

1934   *Crusader* speedboat 24' for Mr Cavanaugh. Motor passenger launch on Sydney Harbour 1934-35.

1935   April- Reported building 2 cruisers and a speedboat. October- building two 29' cruisers for WH Newman of the Railway Dept and Mr Penny of Rockdale. Mr Newman's boat is *Cooboo,* recorded as 26'x9'.

1936   *Adaqua* cruiser 30'x9' for Mr Shields

1936   *Naiad* raised deck cruiser 31' x 9' for C Clarke. In Middle Harbour Sydney in 2004.

1936   Cruiser 27' x 9' for GH Bowra.

1939-1953   Regularly advertised a series of 16'-30' motor boats called the Robinson Playmate in Saturdays' *Sydney Morning Herald* Boating classifieds.

John retired in 1953 and died in 1957. We believe his son Victor ran the yard for several years after that. George continued to build boats after his retirement in 1959.

1964   19' launch *Brit* for himself. Story and pictures p70.

1960's   22' launch *Robbo* with Ron Robinson.

1960's   At least three Sabot-class dinghies for his grandchildren. One, *Propellor* is on display at the ANMM. Possibly three more for Snails Bay Sabot Sailing Club, paid for by benefactor Stan Nicholson.

If anyone has further information about any of these or particularly about other boats built by George and/or John Senior and Junior please get in touch through info@sydneywoodenboatschool.com.au

18-footer *Zanita*, built for W Martin in 1907.
JOHN STANLEY COLLECTION

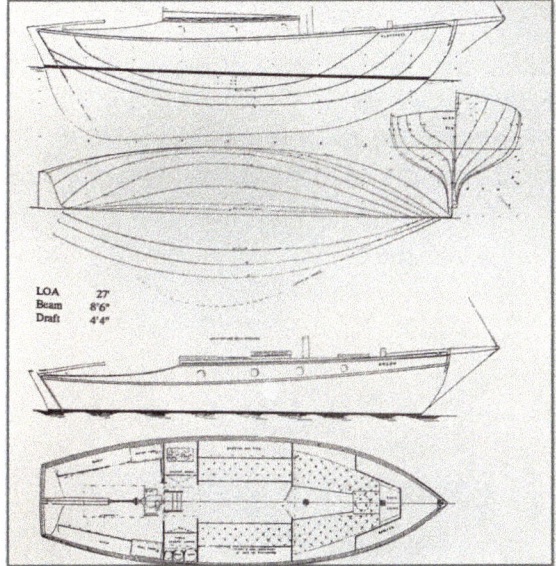

WD Bailey's design *Albatross*, which was used for *Faerie* built in 1928. *Fairie* has a coachhouse, John Robinson may also have built a raised-deck version.
AUSTRALIAN WOODEN BOATS. WOODEN BOAT ASSOC NSW 1993

10-footer *Jean*, 1930. HALL COLLECTION ANMM

John Robinson's shed at 8 School St Balmain East in the late 1940's, where *Britannia* was built in 1919 and where George worked for most of the 1920's and '30's. The slipway starts under the stone wall the two men are standing on at right. The photographer is on the Stannards' wharf next door. The boat looks newly-launched and is probably one of John's Playmate designs.

Britannia as a launch cruises past John Robinson's boatshed (far right behind stern of dinghy). The flagpole is in the centre of the middle level and the house where John and Ella Robinson lived is hidden by the Moreton Bay Fig trees on that level. The big shed at left is Brett's sailmakers (as is the big brick building on top of the hill). Immediately left of Brett's on the waterfront is the lane that was a continuation of Little Ave (now Brett St). Wee Georgie lived in the small weatherboard house on the waterfront just left of the lane from the early 1920's to the late 1950's except for a brief sojourn in Toelle St Rozelle in 1930

All the waterfront properties South (left) of the Robinson shed were demolished in the 1970's for apartment blocks.
PHOTOS FROM ALAN ROBINSON FAMILY

The School St site in 2020. The slipway was where the RIB is moored. George's brother John lived in the stone house centre which was built by shipwright William Burnicle in 1844. Burnicle had about an acre of this land and built several ships to 60 tons there. The shed where *Britannia* was built was approximately where the small timber shed is at left. TRICIA SMITH

Waitangi built in 1922 has been restored by Rick Wood who with his fellow boatbuilder Nigel Shannon also owned and restored the launch *Brit* and were engaged by the ANMM to restore *Britannia* for display. IAN SMITH

Appendix II

Wee Georgie Robinson and his Model Boats

George had a lifelong interest in racing model boats. Talking to Ian Cameron for the Australian Broadcasting Commission's radio series "The Watermen" in 1984 George said:

> *"We used to, when we were kids, we'd go to school, I used to come home and what I used to do, I used to be making models, there was a lot of model sailing in those days, and we used to make 'em, ten inches. We used to race 'em down the beach, down there opposite Mort's Dock there on the beach, and after school we used to have races. Thripence entry you know, and that's how you learned to sail. If you learned to sail a model you can sail a boat, see a model can't sail on its own, you've got to make it sail, you can't get away from Nature. The boat is the fish in the water, your sails are the wings on the birds, that's how your sails should be".*

George claimed this theory was in the forefront of his mind when he designed the 6-footer and 18-footer *Britannia*. He considered that sail balance was very important and claimed he could leave the tiller and walk forward in *Britannia* to check the set of the jib. This checks out in the replica, in steady light breezes to windward and flat water I can let the tiller go for brief intervals.

George claimed he learned a lot about sailing from model boat racing, which he started as a schoolboy. These 2' models are racing off Drummoyne in the 1920's or '30's.
HARRY THOMPSON COLLECTION SFS

Harry Thompson's 2-footer *Advance*, donated by the family to the SFS.
IAN SMITH

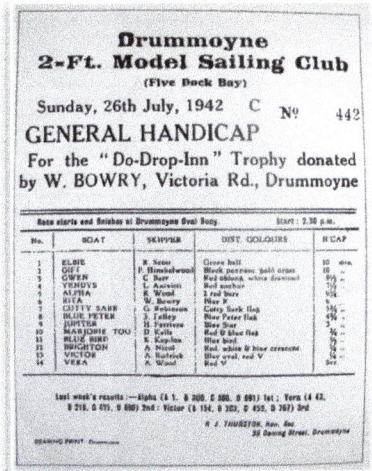

A programme from 1942 shows George in the unusual position of being mid-fleet on handicap.
BALKWELL FAMILY COLLECTION

George probably didn't have time to competitively race his models often while he raced *Britannia* and raised a family, but the extended family gathered in the Christmas holidays at Jack Senior's place at Brooklyn on the Hawkesbury and raced their 2' models (as well as a group of four one-man 10' dinghies they had designed and built).

George started racing with the Drummoyne 2-Ft Model Sailing Club during the War years. The 2-foot models were the most prestigious class (there were classes for 6", 10", 12", 18", 2' (24") and a couple of 36" models). See the Bibliography for Stephen Crewes' book *Sydney's Model Racing Skiffs*.

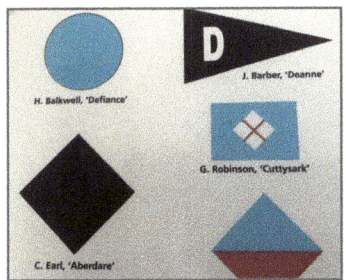

Model sail logos from a programme. George sailed *Cutty Sark* against Horrie Balkwell's *Defiance* among others. BALKWELL FAMILY COLLECTION

The Robinson clan holidayed at Jack's place at Brooklyn at Christmas and would race their 2' models. This one has the family insignia the red 6-pointed star.
ALAN ROBINSON FAMILY PHOTO

Appendix III

Britannia's Crew

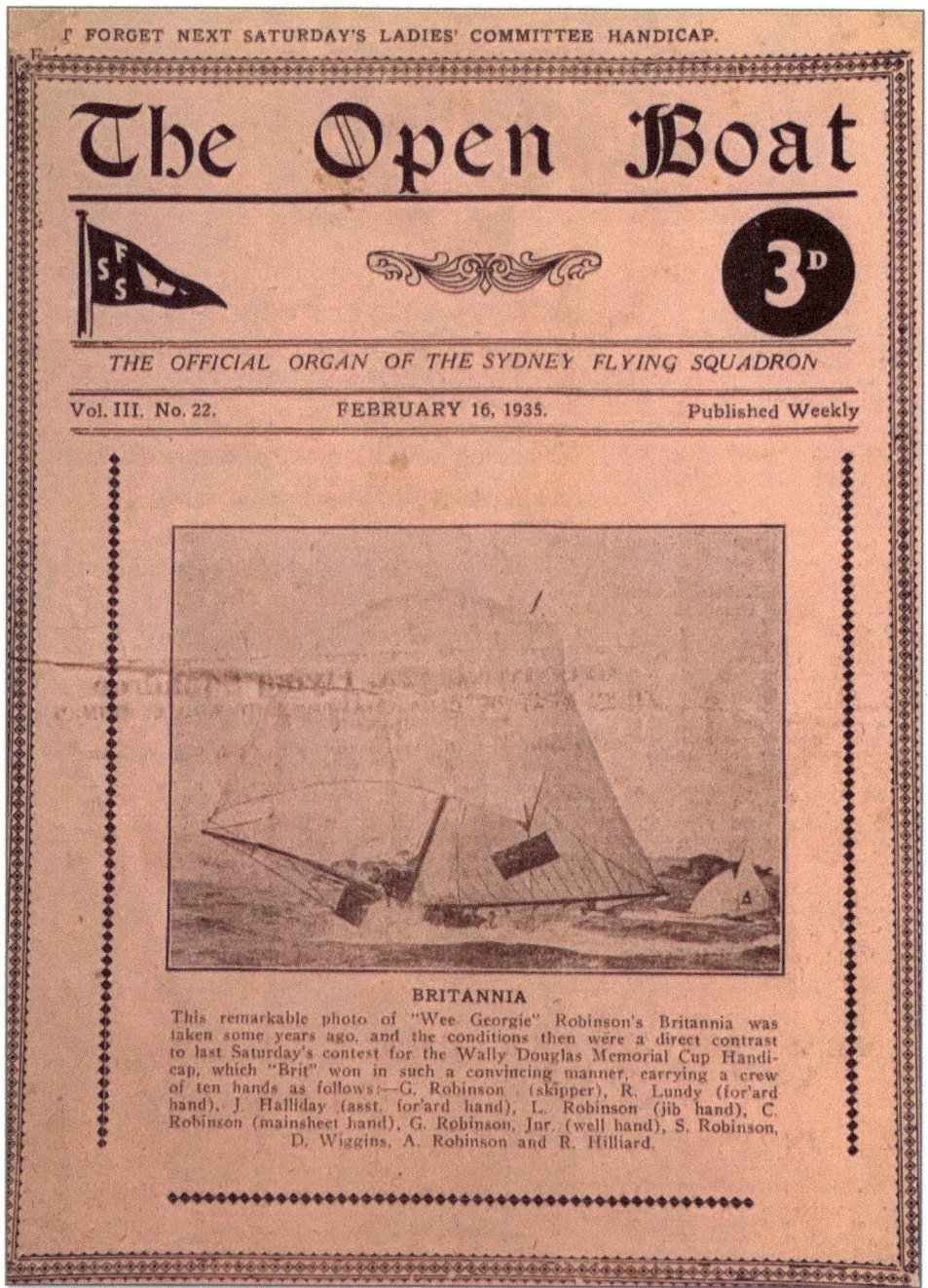

1935 Crew list on race programme. AUTHOR'S COLLECTION

Crew photo probably from the 1929-30 season. Jib hand Les Robinson far left standing, Bob Lundie fourth from left back row, Herb Robson third from right back row, Stan Robinson far right in sports jacket. Front Charlie Robinson reclining, Victor Robinson, John Robinson, Ron, George and unknown. Behind George and Ron with the wide jersey stripes is Roy "Herko" Liston, a non-swimmer famous for sailing with a bag of soil around his neck to keep in touch with land.   ALAN ROBINSON FAMILY PHOTO

Sailing was always a family affair with the Robinsons, often referred to as "the Robbos". Georgie's father Jack (1855-1946) had his brother Charles (1857-1937) as for'd hand until John Junior (1887-1957) started to sail with him, then Charles moved to mainsheet; another brother George (1859-1937) was on the mainsheet early on and later in other roles. Two of Charles' sons sailed with Wee Georgie (1894-1987) for most of *Britannia's* career, Charlie (1894-1971) mostly on mainsheet and Sydney, sometimes posted as Sid (1898-1982), mostly as well hand. Charlie stayed on as *Aberdare's* sheet hand. George (1859-1937) also had a son George Junior (1910-1984) known to the family as "Little Georgie" who sailed in *Britannia* from the early 1930's to early 1940's. Wee Georgie's older brother John Junior sailed as for'd hand from 1919 to 1928 and made occasional appearances after that. Younger brother Les "Fairy" Robinson (1900-1993) was *Britannia's* jib hand until the late 1930's, and occasionally after that, and another brother Stan (1904-1992) sailed often early in the piece.

There were up to 10 Robinsons recorded on board *Britannia* on some days and there was rarely less than 5. Albert "Fatty" Robinson was Georgie's second cousin who sailed in *Britannia* from the early 1930's and also stayed with Georgie on *Aberdare*. Georgie's son Ron (1925-2015) was often on board from the age of 11 in 1936, and John Junior's son Victor also sailed quite a few races. "Latchem" Robinson, another famous Balmain footballer sailed with Georgie occasionally in the early years but was no relation. Other long-term regulars were Jack Halliday, Herb Robson, Mick Russell and of course Bob Lundie.

Crew Lists

The following crew lists have been found in various records, **listed as they were in the original publications.**

12 August 1923
Included in *Britannia's* "athletic crew" were George, Mick Russell, Alf Fraser, Roy Liston, E McFarlane, Tony Russell. *Sunday Times* 12 August 1923

February 1937 Brisbane
G Robinson, R Lundie (Frd), L Robinson (Jib), J Halliday (Asst Frd), C Robinson (Sheet), E Sutcliffe (Well), J Burke, M Russell, J Steele, R Robinson.
Referee 28 January 1937

24 September 1938, opening day, unplaced
George Robinson (skipper), C Robinson (sheet), L Robinson and H Robson (jib), J Robinson and R Lundie (for'ard), G Robinson, junr (well), Sid Robinson, Stan Robinson, A Robinson, R Robinson, F Matthews, W Dunn, J Burke and J Halliday (swingers). *Daily Telegraph,* 24 September 193815 October 1938 Won Admiral Dumaresq Memorial Cup Handicap
Skipper: G Robinson, Forward Hand and Jib Hand: R Lundie, Assistant Frd Hand: J Halliday, Main Sheet Hand: C Robinson, Well Hand: G Robinson (Jun), Swingers: S Robinson, H Matthews, J Halliday (Jun), F Matthews, J Fife, A Martin, K Blackford. RACE AND TROPHY RECORDS, SFS ARCHIVES

Must be a picnic day, late 1920's. Roy Liston holds the cricket bat, Jack Halliday is on his left (our right) in the Tigers jersey. George is centre front, Bob Lundie on George's left. Possibly Sid Robinson front right. JACK HALLIDAY COLLECTION

21 January 1939 Won State Championship
Skipper: G Robinson, Forward Hand: R Lundie, Jib Hand: J Halliday, Main Sheet Hand: C Robinson, Well Hands: G Robinson (Jun), S Robinson, Swingers: F Matthews, H Matthews, K Blackford, J Fyfe, A Martin, J Halliday (Jun). RACE AND TROPHY RECORDS, SFS ARCHIVES

11 February 1939 Won Vaucluse Regatta Handicap
Skipper: G Robinson, Forward Hand: R Lundie, Assistant Frd Hand: J Halliday, Jib Hand: K Blackford, Main Sheet Hand: C Robinson, Well Hands: A Martin, S Robinson, Swingers: F Matthews, J Fyfe, H Matthews, A Johnson. RACE AND TROPHY RECORDS, SFS ARCHIVES

20 January 1940 3rd (pictured below)
G Robinson (Skipper), R.Lundie (Forward Hand), J Halliday (Assistant Forward Hand), H Robson (Jib Hand), G Robinson (Junr), and A Martin (Well Hands), S Robinson (Main Sheet Hand), T O'Donnell, F Matthews, J Fyfe, H Matthews, and C Halliday (Swingers). RACE PROGRAMME, KEN ROBINSON SCRAPBOOK

21 December 1940 Won Wally Douglas Memorial Handicap
Skipper: G Robinson, Forward Hand : R Lundie, Assistant Frd Hand: S Robinson, Jib Hand: T O'Donnell, Main Sheet Hand: C Robinson, Well Hands: G Robinson, H N Moses, Swingers: N Donoghue, E Ryan. RACE AND TROPHY RECORDS, SFS ARCHIVES

20 September 1941 Won Mark Foy Handicap
Skipper: G Robinson, Forward Hand: R Lundie, Jib Hand: R Mulgrew, Main Sheet Hand C Robinson, Well Hands: R Robinson, R Isberg, Swingers: F Matthews, H Matthews, N Moses, K Jefferys. RACE AND TROPHY RECORDS, SFS ARCHIVES

Britannia's crew swing hard in the NSW Championship 20 January 1940. They finished third.
THE SUNDAY SUN AND GUARDIAN, JAN 21 1940, IN JACK HALLIDAY'S SCRAPBOOK IN AUTHOR'S COLLECTION

Bibliography

Most of these books are available from booksellers on the Internet.

Chesterton, Ray: *Tiger, Tiger Burning Bright* Playright, Sydney 2000.
> The story of the Balmain Rugby League Club, in which Wee Georgie Robinson features.

Crewes, Stephen: *Sydney's Model Racing Skiffs* Hippo Books Roseberry NSW 2003.
> Sydney's distinctive model skiffs came in classes from 6" to 2' and bigger. Wee Georgie was a lifelong model sailor.

Elliott, Robin: *Galloping Ghosts* David Ling Publishing, Auckland 2012.
> Thoroughly researched history of Australasian 18-footers 1890-1965 with some great photos.

Jackson, Adrienne; Scully, Steve; and Scully, Veronica: *Setting Sail For The Great War* Sydney Flying Squadron, Sydney 2016.
> The Honour Board of the Sydney Flying Squadron and Sydney Sailing Club contains the names of 149 sailors from these clubs who enlisted for service in World War One before August 1917. The authors have traced the service records of 109 of these men, and put it into the context of the boats they sailed on before the War.

Karas, Chris: *From Fraser to Farah* Chris Karas, Sydney 2009.
> A detailed history of the Balmain Junior League 1908-2008 the Junior branch of the Balmain Tigers Rugby League team with which Wee Georgie Robinson had a long association.

THE AUSTRALIAN MOTOR BOATING AND YACHTING MONTHLY SEPT 1925

Liddle, David: *The Balmain Book* Second Back Row Press, Leura 1985.
   Photos of Balmain characters including Wee Georgie Robinson with *Britannia* and George McGoogan with *Yendys*.

Smith, Ian Hugh *The Open Boat* Sydney Wooden Boat School, Sydney 2017.
   The complete story of where the Aussie 18-footer came from and how it evolved, from its emergence around 1890 to the early 1950's, and a detailed look at how they were built, rigged and sailed. The construction section features the building of the replica of *Britannia*.

Stannard, Bruce: *Bluewater Bushmen* Angus and Robertson, Sydney 1981.
   The first book to celebrate Australian open boats introduced the Hall Collection of glass plate images to the world.

Stephens, Tony with O'Neill, Annette: *Larrikin Days,* Nicholson St Public School P&CA and John Ferguson, Sydney 1983.
   Lots of stories of old Balmain, best part of a chapter on Wee Georgie Robinson.

Toghill, Jeff: *Sydney Harbour of Yesteryear* Reed, Sydney 1982.
   Photos of Sydney Harbour from the Hall Collection including ships, yachts and open boats.

Keriki, Britannia, Mascotte, HC Press II and *NSW,* early 1920's. FAYE MAGNER GIFT TO ANMM

Wahlquist, Asa Karin: *Snails Bay Sabot Sailing Club 1962-1973* WriteLight Pty Ltd, Sydney 2015.

    The story of this junior club that Wee Georgie Robinson had a big role in setting up and running. It tells of a Balmain that has disappeared.

Wooden Boat Assoc NSW: *Australian Wooden Boats* WBA NSW, Sydney 1993.

    A volume of lines plans and construction drawings of classic small boats, including *Britannia*.

Many newspapers were consulted in compiling *Britannia's* history. Some items have come from scrapbooks that have survived, including those of Jack Halliday and Brian Gale of which the author has a copy, and unidentified pages in the collection of the Sydney Flying Squadron. The vast majority of newspapers were studied through trove.nla.gov.au the website of the National Library of Australia, an invaluable resource for researchers.

Videos

The Ian Smith Boats channel on YouTube has the videos *Centenary of Britannia* and *Building Britannia* as well as many videos of the replica sailing. YouTube has many videos of 18-footers from the second half of the 20th century but none from the period when the original *Britannia* was racing due to the restrictive practices of the organisations that control the footage that exists.

Websites

www.openboat.com.au is an extensive and growing depository of images and information about 18-footers and other open boat classes from about 1880 to 1950.

A painting by J. Harvey, 1930's. JACK HALLIDAY COLLECTION

Acknowledgements

The Robinson family was the source of much information and many photos. I had many discussions with the late Ron Robinson, Wee Georgie's son when building the replica. Fay Magner, Wee Georgie's daughter and her daughter Rhonda Magner assisted with information and identification of crew members in photos. Ron's sons Alan and Barry Robinson supplied information and photos. Wee Georgie's nephew Ken Robinson did the same, and Wee Georgie's Great Niece Margaret Gifford allowed access to her family genealogical research.

Bruce and Alan Stannard helped with identification of sites in East Balmain as they had grown up next to Jack Robinson's boatyard. We owe Bruce many thanks for starting the ball rolling with 18-footer research with his book *Bluewater Bushmen*, and for being the driving force in getting the Museum to acquire *Britannia*. Robert Tearne had the original idea to found the Australian Historical Sailing Skiff Association and pioneered the building and sailing of replicas of Aussie open boats. I have had many interesting discussions with Ross Gardner from another East Balmain boatbuilding and sailing family on the community of the time. Robert Halliday from another old Balmain family identified his Grandfather Jack Halliday in photos and provided other photos and Jack's scrapbook.

Britannia's longest set of spinnaker poles was about 39′ (12m) in three sections, though some higher figures have been quoted. FAYE MAGNER GIFT TO ANMM

Asa Wahlquist sent me a copy of her book on the *Snails Bay Sabot Sailing Club* which I didn't have, and the book and discussions with Asa clarified a few matters. New Zealand maritime historian Robin Elliott provided valuable comments and proof-reading. SFS Hon Historian John 'Steamer' Stanley rounded up a great deal of historical material including the Bob Lundie and Harry Thompson collections. David Middleton assisted with George's Rugby League history. Simon Sadubin and Mori Flapan contributed extensively to the list of boats built by Jack Robinson and Wee Georgie in Appendix 1.

I have had many discussions with Rick Wood who has owned and worked on more of Wee Georgie's boats than anyone else, and restored *Britannia* for the Museum, as well as Michael Staples who was Museum Conservator at the time. Both are long-term friends of mine who have contributed many memories and insights.

Britannia and *NSW* have set their biggest spinnakers, ballooners, tops'ls and ringtails in a drifter.
JACK HALLIDAY COLLECTION

David Payne and Daina Fletcher from the Australian National Maritime museum were both involved with the restoration of *Britannia* and assisted with discussions and access to Museum collections. The Museum is to be commended for preserving *Britannia* for posterity and for having the vessel on public display. The late Brian Gale was a sailing legend and a great repository of knowledge of how things were done in the day. I have a copy of his scrapbook. Bob Chapman, Cliff Sutton and Paul Notary assisted with the building of the replica. Racing the replica is a team sport, so thanks go to all who have sailed in her, particularly my loyal regulars.

And my wife Tricia supplied support and provided a sounding board for ideas, as well as her invaluable work on the design and layout of this book. I could not have done it alone. Just like sailing an 18-footer, you need a good bunch of people around you.

Ian Hugh Smith, July 2020.

And now for the next hundred years......

Above: *Britannia* leads the fleet in the early 1920's, just past Steel Point.
HALL COLLECTION ANMM

Below: The replica *Britannia* with the fleet in 2018 a bit further into Rose Bay.
Far left: *Australia IV* with Number 1 on spinnaker, *Scot* obscured behind *Britannia's* ringtail, *Britannia*, *Alruth* and *Tangalooma*, 2018. You can watch the replica fleet race every Summer Saturday, see www.sydneyflyingsquadron.com.au   ADRIENNE JACKSON

PHOTO BY ROWAN FOTHERINGHAM

Ian Hugh Smith has had a forty-plus year career in boatbuilding and boatbuilding education, during which he built upwards of 80 wooden boats from dinghies to yachts. With a long-standing interest in maritime heritage he joined the emerging Australian Historical Sailing Skiff Association which builds, sails and displays traditional Aussie Open Boats and built a 6-footer *Balmain Bug* and 10-footer *Republic* to join the growing replica fleet. In 2001-2 he built the 18-footer replica *Britannia,* the subject of this book, and still sails it every Summer Saturday with the replica fleet at the Sydney Flying Squadron. Researching *Britannia's* history for the Centenary in 2019 through newspapers, photographic collections and discussions with the Robinson family revealed so much material that it became first a video *Centenary of Britannia,* available on the Ian Smith Boats channel on YouTube, and this book. He is the author of *The Open Boat- The Origin, Evolution and Construction of the Australian 18-Footer,* and *Wooden Boatbuilding- The Sydney Wooden Boat School Manuals,* and is the moderator of the websites www.openboat.com.au and www.sydneywoodenboatschool.com.au

www.ingramcontent.com/pod-product-compliance
Lightning Source LLC
Chambersburg PA
CBHW061134010526
44107CB00068B/2933